ONWARD!

The absolute, $_{no}$ $^{B.S}$ raw, ridiculous,
soul-stirring TRUTH about training
for your FIRST MARATHON

BROOK KREDER

ISBN – 978-0-9896831-2-8

MEDICAL DISCLAIMER

This memoir contains general information about medical conditions and treatments. The information is not advice, and should not be treated as such. You must not rely on the information in this memoir as an alternative to medical advice from your doctor or other professional healthcare provider. If you have any specific questions about any medical matter you should consult your doctor or other professional healthcare provider. If you think you may be suffering from any medical condition you should seek immediate medical attention. You should never delay seeking medical advice, disregard medical advice, or discontinue medical treatment because of information shared in this book.

Dedication

To all the people who believed I could when I didn't yet believe for myself.

And to YOU... if you're considering YOUR first marathon. It's a crazy, soulful, hilarious, challenging, bad a**, rugged journey. But I guaranfreakintee – if you want to change your life, this sh*t works.

ONWARD!

Brook Kreder

I never, in my life, thought I'd run a marathon.

And if you knew me, YOU never would have thought I would, either.

In all fairness, I never really cared to chase 26.2 miles. After all, who is dumb enough to say, (out loud, of course), "Oh, heck yeah, man! I'm all kinds of in on beating the hell out of myself for 18 weeks straight in hopes I don't freakin' kill myself on race day."

Not only that, but, "Hey! I'd love to tear up my skeletal structure, lose a toenail or two, give up my coveted weekends and be a bona fide, bat sh*t, white hot mess for the better half of a YEAR."

Yeah, um. That'd be me.

Before you dive in to the blow-by-blow of all things marathon, there are a few things I'd like to confess.

When I decided to hop on the marathon training bus, my life was a f*ing *disaster*.

I've spent the better part of my 30s moving between depressed and completely p*ssed off. I was mostly mad at myself for making crappy choices, and then I'd get depressed about the results of those crappy a** choices.

Trust me, there have been some doozies.

The first terrible idea I had was starting my own business. I suppose there are people on the planet who are designed to be entrepreneurs. At the time, I definitely wasn't one of them. I started my own business about the same time the economy totally blew out. So, as sh*t was burning down before my very eyes, I forced myself to do "whatever was necessary" to make the sale.

Now, before you go there...no, I never traded sex for money.

But my actions did send my moral compass flying clean off its axis. I willingly threw every last boundary I had out the ever-lovin' window. I let my clients run roughshod over me: "You need a ride to the airport? No problem. You want a bunch of sh*t for free? I've got your back.

You need me to pick up your groceries and then swing by and pull the f*ing stitches out of your back? I'm your girl."

Anything for the sale, right?

I got married around the time I started my business, which didn't bode well for anyone.

Here's what I believe: No one teaches you how to be married. Colleges should offer an MBA in all things holy matrimony. This sh*t is hard. Furthermore, no one hands over a "how to" guide for being a wife and a woman. Nor do they share how these two very important roles can coexist peacefully in the same person. So, for the first three years of my "union," I willingly gave away my power. (I honestly thought that's what wives were supposed to do.) I kept my mouth shut. I was a go-along-to-get-along sort of gal. I turned my back on myself and what I knew to be right and true for me. I erased every last boundary in hopes of having a loving, happy relationship with Hubs.

Don't do that.

Here's what I learned: When you give up your boundaries in any area of your life, you lose your soul.

Every time I moved a boundary or one got danced on, stepped over or shoved to the side, I lost a bit of myself. Over time, my self-confidence and self-worth were MIA. I had slowly become a victim in my own life. And the truth is, I had no one to blame but myself.

[Here's where I get empowered.]

I woke up one morning in mid-December (after turning 36) and finally clued in that being a victim looked awful on me.

I needed a way out, so I chose to do something I could control: I decided that something was to train for my first marathon.

Listen. It took me six full years to hit bottom. When I got there, I took a long, hard look around. That's also when Self and I had a come-to-Jesus meeting of the mind.

I said, "Okay Self, remember me? You're in the ugliest, crappiest, darkest place you've ever been in the history of your life. Now, what in the f* are we going to do to get out of here?"

Self shrugged and said, "Run a Marathon."

So, I did.

For me running isn't about pounding pavement and racking up miles. Running is the vehicle I used to heal. Over 18 weeks and a sh*t load break downs, blow outs and damn bad plans along the trail, I found My voice. My heart. My sanity. My truth.

I even found My bad-a**-mother-f*ing swagger.

Running a marathon helped me to reconnect with My *Self*.

And the bonus? I also found my purpose. (Surprisingly, it's to make people laugh and give it to 'em straight! Who knew?)

All this leads me to this book.

Inside, you'll find the blow-by-blow of how I trained for my first marathon. It's a no B.S., daily account of my training woes, mistakes, miles, breakthroughs and more. It's raw, uncensored and loaded with truths and cuss-words. (So if cuss words offend you, this book isn't for you.)

Why did I decide to blog — daily, no less — about this experience?

For one, I wanted a place to tell *this* story. I never intended for anyone else to read or follow the blog; I just wanted somewhere to store my thoughts.

I also wanted a space to tell the freakin' truth. Never once did anyone mention that crazy, unpredictable, mind-blowing sh*t WILL happen to you when you're in training.

And lastly, I blogged because writing every day – even when it was hard and I had no time or no idea what to say -- helped me find my voice.

*Note: You'll see a significant improvement in my writing as the book progresses. If YOU want to be a better writer, commit to pounding it out on your keyboard daily. That sh*t works.*

The bottom line is this: I turned the blog into a book because my readers asked me to.

I sincerely hope you'll love reading this as much as I loved living it.

So, without further ado, let the crazy, soulful journey to 26.2, begin. And be prepared to laugh YOUR ever-lovin' a** off.

ONWARD!

Brook

Brook Kreder
Chief Runner
www.BrookKreder.com

P.S. I'd love to meet you. When you're ready, come over and say hey at www.facebook.com/BrooksFirstMarathon.

P.S.S. Is there an easier way to re-gain control of your life? Maybe. But I always tell people if you want to change your life, run a marathon. The cool part is it's the truth.

P.P.S.S. This book comes with a ton of free resources including, simple, easy to use worksheets, checklists, trainings, etc. Get instant access at www.MarathonTrainingTools.com.

Not All Fitness Centers Are Created Equal

I worked out in a 2-feet-by-3-feet fitness center this morning.

I'm staying in a somewhat dingy Residence Inn. (Sorry, Marriott). The temperature is negative 300, and that's just too damn cold to run outside. I was left with no choice; I was forced to burn up their dreadmill.

To make things worse, the thermostat in that tiny box of fitness was stuck at 712 degrees.

There were no more than three inches between machines, which means there was exactly zero personal space between me and the guy oozing sweat next to me.

That is a terrifying place to be.

I could seriously smell him. (I'm not kidding.)

Through God's grace, I cranked out 3.14 miles and burned 340 calories. All before 6 a.m.

And I surprisingly lived to tell about it.

Welcome to day ONE of my crazy, soulful journey to 26.2. I have no f*ing idea what I'm in for, but I guaranfreakintee it will be good.

All Time Sugar High

I spent three hours yesterday binging on sugar.

My girlfriend Andi invited me over to help make her super secret absolutely to die for no freakin' way you won't get addicted sugar cookies.

They were outrageously good. (As was the homemade cinnamon frosting.)

Here's how it went down…

She had the dough pre-made so I wouldn't pick up the secret of her "secret" ingredient. (Damn it.) But I did get to help roll, cut, bake and decorate those tasty little pieces of art.

While the cookies were baking, she brewed me a fresh cup o' joe. She then proceeded to hand me a HUGE ceramic owl.

Inside?

More homemade hot chocolate than a girl could guzzle in a lifetime.

In addition to my fish-bowl size mug of coffee and hot chocolate goodness, I ate a truckload of cookie dough. Then I devoured two baked cookies loaded with frosting. And finally, a caramel chocolate truffle with sea salt.

My stomach was begging for mercy.

Hands down this is the most sugar I've ever ingested, in one setting, in my entire freakin' life.

But, I guaranfreakintee when I'm banging out 10 miles tomorrow, I won't feel one damn bit bad about my binge.

I'm thinking of sneaking back in to Andi's house while they're on vacation to steal the recipe. Problem is, if I made them at home I'd eat every last one. By myself.

Worst. Idea. Ever.

Today marked my first outdoor run of the year.

It was 52 degree at 1 p.m. and the weather was dy-no-mite.

Even with the sun at my back, I still managed to learn several ridiculously important lessons. (All of which are good to know as I embark on my training adventure.)

Lesson #1: Never, EVER head out for any type of run within an hour of eating.

Think esophageal mayhem. 'Nuff said.

Lesson #2: I will never be an afternoon runner. Period.

I have complete and total clarity that I'm an a** crack of dawn kind of girl. No exceptions.

Lesson #3: Running outside preferred.

I haven't been able to run outside because temperatures have been in the single digits. (I'm a hearty girl from Nebraska but that's too damn cold.) I will take an outdoor run over the dreadmill any day.

Lesson #4: If your heart's not in it, you're f*ed.

I've been uber emotional for the last few weeks, which has deeply affected my long runs. (I haven't figured out a viable workaround yet...so I'll keep putting in the miles anyway.) If I find the cheap, easy, totally doable solution I'll be sure to share.

Here's my wisdom for today:

Run when you want to. Run when you don't. Run when you're sad. Run when you're pissed.

Run when you're feeling hella good.

It's all a part of showing up and proving to yourself you can and will do this...regardless of the circumstances.

Cross Training Is A B*tch

And she snuck up on my BIG time yesterday.

I've been laying out my training schedule for the next four months and it includes one to two days a week cross training (CT). While my final schedule has yet to be determined, I am proud I'm at least planning for it.

The idea behind CT is to work "other" muscles groups in your body to balance your strength and endurance. (You know, because simply running 20 miles isn't enough.) The experts say CT will leave you better prepared on race day. As I'm new to this, I have no other choice than to believe them.

Hubs and I headed out for a death march on our bikes. It was almost 60 degrees, which was a freakin' TREAT coming off a 4 degree high earlier in the week.

I have to be honest. I was a tad bit nervous about hitting the trail.

Two weeks ago, on the very same trail, a mean-spirited, a** hole of a dog ran up to me, while I was riding, and bit me on the f*ing ankle.

Not only did that three pound, spineless, four-legged jerk bite two symmetrical holes in my favourite pair of socks, but he broke *skin*.

In two places.

Thankfully, yesterday's ride was without incident.

That said, after a 10-mile, post-nacho run yesterday and a 24-mile death march on my bicycle, my legs are cryin'. (Think John Wayne swagger up in here. It's bad; worse than you can imagine.)

Here's my take away: Training for my first marathon is going to take everything I've got.

And then it's going to take MORE.

I don't yet know enough to be worried. But I probably should be.

What the Experts Don't Share

Turns out, training for a marathon is an a** load of work.

It's a pretty cool thing when you finally commit to running your first marathon. You get excited. Inspired. Over the top committed. You're ready to pound pavement and burn the world down. The problem is, no one pulls back the curtain and tells you just how much effort this takes.

At least no told me…maybe I missed the memo?

After last weekend's series of a** busting activities, my freakin' legs today are still crying.

This both surprises and scares me.

I'm surprised because I ran two half marathons last year and my legs never felt this bad.

I'm scared, because after my 24 mile bike ride, I realized I will have to run even farther than that on race day.

As I mentioned, this week I've been fine tuning my marathon training calendar. While I've left the weekdays somewhat open (I'm planning between 3-6 miles 4-5 days per week), my long runs are etched in stone.

I'm here to tell you, this simple exercise got me all kinds of terrified. It evoked a ton of self-doubt. Can I do this? Should I? Who am I to say I'll run a marathon? Maybe it was a lousy idea to tell people I was doing this. If I back out now, no one will think less of me, right?

But I'm not a quitter. And I always honor my word.

So ONWARD I go.

My friend told me I'd likely lose a toenail or two on this adventure. It's going to get ugly 'round here.

A Girl's Power Tools

I am a proud, card-carrying member of two celebrated clubs.

The first is the Dyson Club. (You know, the swanky vacuums that suck every last piece of terrible nonsense out of your carpet.)

And I just joined the Vita Mix Club.

I've had my eye on a Vita-Mix Blender for a long freakin' time. They're an investment to be sure.

After my lunchtime Mexican-food blowout last week, I knew it was time to add a few tools to my nutritional toolbox. Enter the Vita Mix.

The day after the beautiful, ginormous box arrived from Amazon, I trekked to the grocery store and laid down $127 for fruits and veggies.

The skeptic in me was thinking, "Is there any way on God's green earth I'll be able to eat all of this? I was also thinking, "What will this do to my f*ing colon?" but I'll save THAT story for another day.

The hell-bent, motivated, marathoner-wanna-be in me knew I'd give eating these fruits and veggies my best effort.

So I'm on day two of mean smoothies for breakfast. (And so far, no colon blow. Although I will say, add a ton of veggies. It will help keep your blood sugar stable.)

Honestly, I'm kind of impressed with myself for crafting such a tasty solution. A nice aside is that my body feels happy, too.

Happy enough to chase my first-ever 14-mile run this weekend.

Which happens to be the farthest I have ever run in the history of my existence.

Today, I'm celebrating being proactive, power tools, and new personal bests.

40 Minutes of Silence

I wanted to share what I saw this morning.

I watched a sunrise that took my breath away.

Today is a cross-training/rest day, so Midas (my dog) and I headed out at 5 a.m. for a brisk walk. For the first time in a long time, I left my iPod Shuffle on the counter.

I wanted to get down with the good Lord.

I usually talk "at" God.

I praise him for all that's new and good. I ask for forgiveness of my many, many sins. I then take BOLD action and make requests for other people. (And myself, of course.) I wrap up by trying to turn my entire day over to Him.

But rarely do I *listen*.

That's why once a week, I make a conscious effort to ditch the tunes and plug in to what God might be trying to say to me.

I love these days. No music. No mindless chatter. No busting my a** running up a crazy hill.

I just get quiet.

I have never heard from him in a way that makes sense in the human realm.

But more often than not, the silence is gift enough.

I know he's there. I know he's in this with me. I know he's got my back.

I know it's by his amazing grace I'm training for this race. And it's by his grace alone that I will cross the finish line in a few months.

I have no doubt he'll be with me every step of the way.

50 Ways to Leave Your Lover

I freakin' LOVE Paul Simon.

I have several of his Top 10 hits on my shuffle, so he croons to me six days a week. I'm a lucky, lucky girl.

My favorite song?

Late in the evening.

I love the lyrics. But what I really dig is the groove. The soul. The way it makes me want to move. (Even when my legs are protesting.)

I've been on the hunt for some new songs to add to my shuffle. If you have an iPod, mp3, whatever, you know how tired songs can get. And fast.

I've listened to Ricky Martin belt out "She Bangs" well over 140 times. Don't hold it against me – I use to love that song. Now? Not so much.

I've allocated $100 of my first marathon-training budget to the iTunes store. So, last night I added Kelly Clarkson, Ke$ha and two other people I don't remember.

As the Shuffle was syncing, I looked at my stats. I have six hours and 52 minutes of music on this tiny piece of equipment. 103 songs. Which is hard to believe because it seems like I'm listening to the same bloody tunes over and over.

I bought my Shuffle a year ago for $50 bucks. And I downloaded a few of my all-time favorite songs. Think tunes from Jo Dee Mesina, Eric Clapton, Katy Perry, the works.

I remember the first time I listened to my cherry-picked play list. I was in complete shock. There's something very magical about choosing only the best songs…without having to buy the entire album.

Now I'm a self-declared iTunes addict. (Which, I am sure, Apple is counting on.)

The only thing left for me to wish for is diamonds on the soles of my shoes.

I'd Pay Double

I'm no spring chicken.

Don't get me wrong. I don't feel old per say, but I'm not 21 anymore. I'm 36... and with that age comes a lot of hard-earned lessons and wisdom. And a hell of a lot more pain, too.

This morning I'm off to see the chiropractor.

I used to be very reactive in my approach to chiropractic. The only time I'd think to schedule an appointment was if 1) If I couldn't freakin' *walk* or 2) My neck was locked in one position.

It took me awhile to figure out chiropractic care can help. What I've learned through training, and by having scheduled, bi-monthly appointments, is that proactive feels much better.

I'm on his table for about five minutes.

In that time, he yanks on my legs. Punches the bottom of my feet. Twists my neck around backwards. Works my calves. My shins. And cracks my back from here to Shinola.

I always break a sweat. (Which is kind of weird, but I think it's my body crying for help.)

I walk out of his office feeling 21. (Nice, right?)

He's worth every stinkin' penny.

I plan to see him 10 times before race day. Unless sh*t gets messy, of course. Then it will be more. Whatever it takes... that's my motto.

Can you train for a marathon without a chiropractor on your team? Probably.

But I have no intention of finding out.

I don't want you to think I'm not putting in the miles. Today was three miles outside at 4:45 a.m. The moon was almost full, which surprised me because I don't feel bitchy. Tomorrow, I'm up for 12 miles...stand by.

Chafing: To Rub So As To Wear Away

Day 10

This is about as pornographic as it's going to get.

My strange, unexplainable desire to document the entire "first marathon training process" propels me to complete and utter transparency. So here we are.

Instead of the song, "I Fought the Law," think "I fought the bra and the bra won. I fought the bra and the bra won."

There is a beautiful, bold, scathing red line across my upper belly where my sports bra tried to saw me in half this morning.

Good news is…the bra was unsuccessful.

The bad news? It f*ing hurts.

Which brings me to the topic of chafing.

I didn't experience any "wearing away of the skin" while training for my half marathons last year. So it burns my a** just a bit that it's already on the list of things to avoid. (Especially this early in the game.)

I always gain new wisdom on long-runs, and today's 12.5-mile throw down was no exception. Here's what I learned:

1) Not all sports bras play fair.

2) Make sure your water bottles actually have water IN them before you place them in your belt. (Yes, I carried empty bottles today. Ridiculous.)

3) I am comforted by the camaraderie on the trail at 6 a.m. No one gives a sh*t how you look, and honestly, they don't look that great either.

It was 34 degrees when I headed east toward the sun. I ran a new leg of trail, which breaks up the monotony. The sun warmed my back down the home stretch, which always fills my soul.

Sans my biting sports bra, today was a really good day.

I made homemade cinnamon rolls last night and I savored every last sticky-sweet-calorie-loaded bite.

My Accountability Buddy

My dog probably has more miles on him than most.

His name is Midas. He's a 100-pound, light-haired golden retriever. He's my alarm clock. My muse. My six-day-a-week running companion.

I've never pushed him past 4 miles. (He'd probably make it, but it's my job as Mom to worry.) Between running and walking, he's logged 45 miles this month.

Without fail, he's up between 4 a.m. and 5 a.m. every single day.

Here's how the rooster crows at my house:

Midas walks over to my side of the bed and starts panting. He uses his nose to nudge my elbow. He backs up a few steps, shakes his a**, and comes in again.

Ten minutes after the theatrics begin, my a** is stumbling towards the closet to get dressed.

Midas refuses to let me skip a single day of exercise. Not only is he doing his part to keep me fit…but there are times he's probably kept me safe.

A few months back, when there were more dark hours in a day than light, I invested in two headlamps. One fits snugly over my stocking cap…the other clasps firmly around his neck.

Truth be told, I got damn tired of near misses, (cars, animals and whatnot), in my neighborhood first thing in the morning.

I'm 1000 percent positive we look utterly ridiculous.

But, as the law in my life reads, "Ugly sells" before 6 a.m.

I can always count on Midas for a dozen or so pee breaks every morning, which makes my runs much easier. I swear to you this dog pees on every turd he can find. Probably some pretend turds, too.

Body vs. Mind

Day 12

I realized something important about myself today.

Of all things marathon, rest days are the hardest. Not because my body doesn't need the break...it so freakin' does. They're hard because my *mind* throws a fit.

This weekend I ran 12.5 miles Saturday and 3 miles on Sunday. I also stirred in a four-mile hike with a 800 ft. climb Sunday afternoon.

Today my body is SCREAMING -- Love! Rest! Healthy Food! A Nap! (It's also trying to twist my arm for a massage. Truth be told, it just might get its way.)

My mind is SCREAMING -- You shouldn't take a day off! You won't finish the marathon! No rest for the weary! Get off your freakin' a** sister and move! (It's crazy what the mind does to you.)

Part of training is letting your body heal between runs.

Which means resting your weary bones and muscles so they can come back stronger. Better. Faster.

I've been chewing on why I don't want to give my body a rest. It's something to do with my self-worth being tied to my level of productivity. (I.e. how much I can accomplish in a day.)

I don't have any answers. I just wanted to share my insights. And I'm also curious if anyone else in the world feels the same.

I talk a lot about "Going PRO" in my business. I've also said I'm going PRO in my life...with a marathon being the vehicle.

Part of going PRO is doing sh*t you don't want to in the short-term so you can reach your long-term goals.

So today, I'll rest.

And I'll do my best to like it.

A Hybrid Approach

I woke up to a thousand inches of snow this morning.

I'm terrible at gauging how many inches actually fell. It's probably around 4 but I'll call it 12.

The white fluffy stuff wasn't enough to deter my run completely, but Midas and I were definitely forced to take a hybrid approach.

We made a deal:

Run the flats and climbs – and walk down the hills.

I seriously have NO interest in busting my a** or breaking my arm, especially early in the morning. Not to mention that any type of serious injury would derail my marathon training schedule – absolutely not.

There is something very magical about being the first person to step into fresh snow. It only happens a dozen or so times a year so we enjoy every solitary second.

Later in the day, Midas and I went back out for a brisk walk. The snow was starting to fall – it looked like small round white pebbles.

While trekking around the neighborhood, I held out my hand to see how much snow I could catch.

I had a few pieces hit my glove and bounce out, but I was surprised at how little stuck.

Then I stood still.

And the snow flocked to my glove. (And stayed.)

My lesson in that moment was:

Sometimes you have to STOP running and just stand still so the good things can find you.

Running = Scary Business?

I never wanted to be a freak about safety.

But the time has come for me to get smart (and real!) about what's going on in the world.

Safety is now top-of-mind because of an incident in Denver last week. A woman walking a local trail was sexually assaulted.

When I Googled "sexually assaulted," I found the definition to be broad and vast. Merriam-Webster says it's illegal sexual contact that usually involves force upon a person without consent. It seems to be a catch-all phrase for everything from touching to the absolutely terrible.

In reality, I'll probably never be 100 percent safe when I'm out running. (I run at zero dark thirty. There are very few people around, which is good and bad.)

So here's what I've decided:

1) I'm hiring a support person. That way someone will always have water, fuel and first aid ready should I need it. They will also know exactly where I am and where I'm supposed to be for the duration of my long-runs.

2) I dug out my mace. I pity the fool who makes me use it…and I pray I never spray myself.

3) I'm taking a self-defense class ASAP. I now consider this a non-negotiable part of my "git-er-done" strategy.

I sincerely hope safety isn't something I'll have to talk about often.

But it's definitely worth some thought.

Because scary or not, getting smart about safety will serve me long after I run my first marathon.

I put up 4.3 miles this morning in 5 degree weather. My face was frozen for a good half hour after. Good news is I hear it's the cure all for wrinkles.

A Ridiculously Simple Ritual

At the first of the year, I started an exercise journal.

I heard somewhere that's I'd probably run between 350 - 500 miles to train for the marathon. Now I know it's true.

I happen to love numbers. Anything I can measure and/or track, especially in business, I'm all in. So I thought I'd do the same with training.

Since January (and the beginning of my marathon training), I've been writing down every last bit of exercise. Think runs, walks, hikes and bike rides.

After my first 30 days, here's where the numbers shook out:

Ran: 116 miles	Walked: 26 miles
Hiked: 4 miles	Biked: 24.5 miles
Elliptical: 2	Midas: W/R/H: 56.5 miles

That's 211.5 miles of movement.

In 30 freakin' days.

No wonder I can eat a house. (I'm hungry all the time.)

I've made a ritual of writing down my numbers daily. It's a ridiculously simple step but it keeps me motivated.

Right now, every little bit helps.

Midas and I put up 4.3 miles this morning. It may have been above freezing, but barely. Tomorrow, I'll taper down for my 14-miler on Saturday. Prayers welcome.

FREE RESOURCE: Download your Free Fast-Action Activity Journal at www.MarathonTrainingTools.com.

My Caloric Confession

I am so pissed at myself.

I was wide-awake at 2:30 a.m. with heartburn like a mofo. (And not a chance-in-hell of going back to bed.) So I got up and cleaned the house until 5 a.m., then grabbed Midas and we hit the road for our daily dose of running.

Here's where I start blabbing my indiscretions and confessions...

I mentioned yesterday I'm starving all the time. And usually, I'm prepared for starving with some healthy snacks on stand-by.

But last night I got home late. I threw a frozen pizza in the oven. And when I finished off just over half of that cheese-loaded-round-piece-of-goodness, I still wanted more.

So I made strawberry shortcake and loaded it to the gills with butter, sugar and fruit.

I probably consumed 2,000 calories and 50 grams of sugar in 30 minutes. Please don't judge... I was desperate.

I did the same thing earlier this week at Outback Steakhouse. I thought I'd celebrate how far I've come by chowing on a half a plate of cheese fries. I paid dearly for that splurge, too.

It's been a tough week on the nutrition front. I'm trying to find the balance between carb-loading and blow out. My body is changing so much and so fast that frankly; I'm doing a lousy job of keeping up.

But no more.

I'm back in the saddle. I'm headed to the grocery store today. And it's (mostly) clean-living for me from here on out. Because having your a** handed to you by your own damn self just plain sucks.

Tomorrow is 14 miles. Last time I attempted 14, I ran 7 out, turned around, got a massive side cramp and walked all the way back to the car. We'll see how sh*t shakes out.

Lattes, Lessons and Layin' It Down

I saw a Starbucks at the seven-mile turnaround today.

It took everything I had not to go inside and snuggle up with a non-fat, skinny anything. But I know better. If I stopped in the middle of a long run, I would never make it back to the car. So I passed. But barely.

As I flew by this roasted-cocoa-bean-mouth-watering-mecca-center at a whopping 6 miles per hour, I couldn't help but think, "Good freakin' night. They aren't kidding when they say there's a Starbucks on every bloody corner."

It was a big day for me. I put up 14.33 miles and burned 1,540 calories. It was BIG because I've never run more than 13.1 in my *entire* life.

Today, I created a new normal.

A part of me is like, "Yeah, yeah, and if it were race day you'd still have 11.9 miles to go." (I know, WTF.) But the other part is doing a very sexy, very happy get-down-on-it-sister dance.

Because two years ago, I couldn't run five minutes. A year ago, I couldn't run five miles. And today, I put up what I consider to be monster number. And I'm proud of myself.

Here are my long-run lessons of the week:

1) For the first time ever I ran a few miles without headphones. The sound of my feet hitting the pavement made me feel grounded.

2) I carried mace. And a few times I did put my thumb on the trigger. (I only worried once that I might spray myself.)

3) I lubed up my chafed area from last week – it worked!

4) I carry my cell phone in a Ziploc sandwich bag stuffed between my girls. It scratches my chest up something fierce. I need a better plan.

In full-disclosure, I cried a few times today. I cried in gratitude for all the people supporting me on this journey. I cried to Neil Diamond's song

"AMERICA." And lastly, I cried near the end because 14 miles is a new personal best.

To skipped lattes, not-too terrible lessons and layin' down a PB.

Hell yes, I'm keeping with custom and heading out for a big, fat margarita.

Be Believers

My BFF hung with me last weekend.

She spent 11 hours shopping on Saturday. Who the f* does that? Thank God I opted out. I would have killed myself. Or killed her. Or have been forced to take a cab home. It would have been ugly, regardless.

Tiffine has been my soul sister for 10 years. She holds a space for me to play big. Be bold. Take risks. Aim high. Chase every single last stinkin' thing I want in this life.

She's also the person I'd call if I needed to bury a body or be bailed out of jail. You know what I mean. She's THAT type of friend.

She whole-heartedly believes in me.

On my run this morning, I thought about why I started training for a marathon in the first place. After all, who intentionally tries to run 26.2 miles consecutively with no promise of fame or financial reward?

Here's the truth: I started because a few close friends believed I could.

I'll never forget. My girlfriend Andi and I were out to lunch a few months ago chatting about running, training, upcoming races and goals. Toward the end of the conversation, she looked me dead in the eye and said with total authority, "You can run a marathon. I believe you can."

I took Andi's belief and chewed on it for a long time. Because while Andi's believe was awesome, I knew I had to believe too.

My wisdom today is it only takes one.

One single, solitary person who believes you can _____.
(Enter your words here.)

And their belief ignites a series of unexplainable, unimaginable events in your life that ultimately lead to YOU believing, too.

Today isn't about how many people believe in me. It's about what we can accomplish in the world if we believe in each other. None of us, not me, not you, not anyone, has enough people in our corner cheering, "Hell Yes! You can do anything you choose!"

So my challenge for all of us today is to be that.

Join me in creating a movement of belief.

Because other people need it.

You will love it.

And the world we live in today deserves it.

Midas and I ran 3 miles this morning – and we have a 4-mile hike planned this afternoon. Oh yes, and I'm back in the saddle on the food front (sans yesterday's margarita). Woot!

This Morning I Said F* It

My favorite pair of jeans has been in my Goodwill pile for months.

When I bought them a few years ago, they were just a little too tight. (Am I the only one who has ever done this?!?!) But I thought, "What the hell, I'll figure out a way to squeeze into these suckers, (somehow!), in the next few months."

It's been two years.

And seriously, I almost gave them away last week to a very lucky soul who loves bling plastered all over their butt cheeks. (Think rhinestones everywhere... these jeans scream cowgirl/rodeo/I'm f*ing hot.)

So this morning, I'm getting dressed in my closet and I stare longingly at those jeans. And I decided, f* it. I'm trying them on. So I did. And they slid right up with a tiny bit of room to spare.

I heard the angels sing. God came down, patted me on the head and said, "Way to go girl. I've always had a plan for you and these jeans..."

This is an awesome aside of training for a marathon. (But I am wondering if I'll bulge back out of them by July.)

On the flip side...

I'm burning though Botox so fast my pocket book can't keep up. I've been getting Botox in my forever-wrinkled-forehead for *years*. It should last 12 weeks. Today I'm on week 5, and it's messy up in here.

So I have a decision to make. Up my frequency, or let it all hang out. And honestly, I'm kind-of leaning towards letting it all hang out. Because there's something very honest about letting sh*t be what it will be.

To killer skinny jeans, showing your age and going au natural.

*I did hire a support person this week. Deets to come – the story is f*ing hilarious.*

Book of Awesome

Last year, I started a Book of Awesome.

A Book of Awesome is a magical notebook/journal and/or sketchpad.

Inside you chronicle five things (daily) that are uber awesome about being YOU. You know, like what's new and good in your life. What you're thankful for. Why it's so damn amazing to be you.

My girlfriend Paula gave me the idea so I would develop a ritual of gratitude.

There are times in your life when it's so freakin' easy to focus on the bad that you have to dig deep for the awesome. That's where a ritual like this can help.

I revisited my Book of Awesome this morning. Here's a secret peek of what's inside:

- Saying Yes! to me.

- A 40-minute nap. (Sure wished this happened more...)

- Reconnected with an old friend. (Sure wish this happened more, too!)

- I am healthy. I am free and able to run my dog in my neighborhood.

As I flipped back through the pages, I was surprised at how much gratitude I had for the little things. Yeah... there were some heroic acts in there, too. But overall, I usually wrote about the simple things in my everyday life that make me awesome.

Today my page will say:

- A strong run (uphill!) with Midas at 4:30 a.m. The wind was blowing so hard it choked me... WTF?!)

- For my dentist -- a man who can see me with my mouth wide open, (and all of its imperfections), and dig in anyways.

- A superstar phone call with a client, whom I both respect and adore.

- For a phone call with an old friend about a new project.

- For the journey I'm on for the next 100+ days. And the fact that you're with me.

This is going to be awesome.

I've lost a dozen pair of running gloves over the last year… and they are freakin' expensive. Today, I "found" a lost glove tucked in the back seat of my car. Now THAT is awesome.

This Stinks To High Hell

Day 21

This morning Midas and I had a near run-in with Pepe le Pew.

Two and a half miles into our run, I could smell something was amiss. One tenth of a mile later, (mile 2.6), I became concerned. At mile 2.7, I completely freaked-the-f*-out.

Here's why: Midas is no stranger to skunks.

Last summer, he was sprayed two times in five freakin' days. Just consider his hair! It's thick and there's way too damn much of it. I can tell you from experience it takes months and months to get the stink off of him.

That's why at mile 2.7, we put on the brakes, entirely.

I leaned down (toward Midas) and took a good whiff.

Nothing.

One tenth of a mile later (you can see how fast we're running, right?) we stopped again because I couldn't shake the smell. I swear it was like the skunk crawled right up in my nose and let 'er rip. I took another whiff.

Nothing.

And of course, for good measure, I leaned in one last time.

All clear.

I could smell that pesky skunk the rest of our 4 mile run. Which is probably a damn good indicator that I breathe way too heavily through my nose.

Today, I'm celebrating sidesteps, a strong sniffer and not seeing a skunk.

Midas has been super pokey lately. I took him to the vet this week. They think he may have a thyroid problem. (He's gained 15 pounds in 6 months and he's putting up some massive miles.) I'll keep you posted.

She's Packing Heat

The Brook's First Marathon team expanded by one this week.

I know. It seems crazy more than one person will be involved in training for my marathon. Who knew?

A few weeks ago, I decided to get mindful about safety. Part of my safety strategy included hiring a support person to keep track of me while I'm out pounding pavement.

I seriously wondered if there was anyone in the world crazy enough to meet me at the a**-crack of dawn every Saturday for 14 weeks. You know, to haul water, fuel and first-aid. Or, to call the freakin' police if I go missing.

So, I posted a part-time contract position on Craigslist. Surprisingly, I got 20 responses.

I fast-tracked the process and went right to in-person interviews. (It was important to me that we gel, especially since we'll be spending a lot of hours/miles together.)

I fell in love with D.R.

We met for lunch and I knew instantly she was compassionate, nurturing, interested, thoughtful and trustworthy. Come to find out, she's also exceedingly knowledgeable about cooking and nutrition. (A huge plus, considering the caloric sh*t storm I've created.)

Oh yeah, and she has her concealed weapons permit, which is another way to say she's packing heat. Did I mention I love her?

We start our journey together this Saturday. It is a shorter run for me, 10 miles, which gives us a chance to figure sh*t out.

A small piece of me feels guilty about having this much support.

Seriously. I've yet to meet another first-time marathoner who has paid a support person. Maybe this will start a movement.

But the super-smart-safety-conscious-marathoner-wanna-be in me said f*
that.

I want to do this well, do it safely, and put this monster dream to bed on
my terms.

*It snowed here last night, so Midas and I walked a few miles this
morning. It was okay by me. I got to leave my shuffle on the counter
again and just "listen."*

*FREE RESOURCE: Download the Craigslist ad for a PT support person
at www.MarathonTrainingTools.com.*

Five Peeps, Two Dogs and A Fan

Day 23

I'd like to start by thanking the City and County of Denver.

For building me my very own, world-class running trail all the way through town. Seriously, at 6:30 in the morning in *February*, there isn't another soul to be seen. I literally saw five people and two dogs in two hours. Awesome, 'eh?

This works for me on so many levels:

- No one sees how *interesting* I look without make-up.

- I never worry about being slammed from behind by a cyclist.

- I can run anywhere I choose, at any speed I choose, and no one is *watching*.

All that said, here's how today's 11.68 mile run shook out:

While driving to the trailhead, I saw two young guys in wheelchairs rolling themselves UP a fairly steep hill. (Their arm strength totally inspired me.) And in that moment, I offered up thanks for having the physical ability to train for a marathon.

Today was also D.R.'s first day. She's a superstar.

Not only was she waiting for me at every rendezvous location, but she never failed to roll down her window and shout out, "Woot-woot sister, keep truckin'!"

It's a kick-a** feeling to have a fan, even if I do pay her. Don't tell her I told you, but I think she hit the McDonald's drive-through between meet-ups. I'd have done the same damn thing given the chance.

I also gave my new sports bra a go.

After my near death experience with chafing last week, I went on the hunt for better options.

To say I was leery of my new contraption from Lululemon is an understatement. Now? I'm a believer.

And finally, near the end of my run, I noticed an unmarked white vehicle. And you know what they say about unmarked vehicles, especially vans.

So I pulled out my phone. (From between the girls.) Slipped off the Ziploc bag. (Hell yes, I'm still on the Ziplocs.) And snuck right up to it. I needed to know the driver's seat was empty before I snapped the picture, right? It was, so game on.

I took a quick picture and ran like wildfire back to the trail.

Even if I did get caught, I knew D.R. was only a few hundred yards away. And because she has her concealed weapons permit, I knew my a** was covered.

Back on the trail, I was in stitches. (Think laughing my head off.) Because I totally freakin' crack myself up. And I'll do whatever it takes to make a long run fly by.

The GPS stopped working today so I'm not sure of my exact mileage. It was somewhere between 10 to 11 miles. I wonder if Mercury is in retrograde?!?!

Definitely A First

This morning, Midas ran like he owned the road.

I don't have to tell you how pissed he gets on Saturdays when I head out solo for my long runs. That said, he does his best to pay me back for my indiscretions on Sundays.

Last night, I was thinking I only have about 25 pounds on that dog.

But he has 4-legs and sits low to the ground. So when he says stop, we stop. And when he says, "Get your a** in gear Mom," I have no choice but to fall in line.

My intention was to do six miles this morning. Instead, we cobbled together three and added a few weights to the mix.

Post-run, I head downstairs (where my weights wait for me) and remember I hadn't yet grabbed the dirty sheets off the bed from the company earlier in the week.

(Here's where it's important to note: I still had my shuffle on and buds in my ears.)

As I'm peeling the pillows from their cases, static electricity got the best of me. And shocked the INSIDE of my freakin' ears.

What the f*!

I stood there for a minute to make sure I hadn't peed my pants.

That I still had use of my *faculties.*

It was definitely a first.

Good news is, I'm fine. Wonders never cease.

I plan to hit up a few running stores this week for some new gear. I've had the same long underwear for years… it's ancient.

100 Pounds of Effort

My good friend Tom once told me …

"Brook, you wake up every single day with 100 pounds of effort. No more. No less. And it's up to you to decide how to allocate your pounds."

(He mentioned this when I was in freak-out mode, while chasing my MBA. Crazy how it still applies.)

Last year, I put my brave girl pants on and walked in to a running specialty store to try on shoes. It was the first time I took my running seriously enough to be fitted for the *right* shoes instead of winging it at the sporting goods store.

The sales clerk was dynamite.

And when I first met her, she happened to be training for her 6th freakin' marathon.

The curious side of me started firing questions about her experience. The one thing she said that I'll always remember…

"When you train for a marathon, there's always a *cost*. You're always forced to give something up."

Smugly (and to myself) I didn't *believe* her.

Hey, when I met Collette, I had only ever run a half marathon. And yeah, the training schedule for a half is kind of rigorous, but totally manageable. How much harder could it be to train for a full?

I believe her now.

You see, my ego wants me to think I'm Superwoman, that I can do everything at the expense of nothing.

But, I know that's no longer true because I am giving things up:

- Time with friends.

- Timely responses to emails.

- Marketing my business.

- A leisurely walk with my neighbor.

- My coveted vodka tonics.

The list goes on, but you catch my drift.

I'm not sharing this because I'm sorry about the sacrifice. I'm not. I'm sharing this because right now, I am choosing how I allocate my 100 pounds, and a huge percentage of it happens to be going to training.

Muhammad Ali said it best, *"I hated every minute of training, but I said, 'Don't quit. Suffer now and live the rest of your life as a champion."*

That's my plan.

It was 7 degrees this morning when Midas and I hit the road. Brrr. We conquered a monster hill – another first.

Feels Like -14 Degrees

F* it was cold this morning.

And there ain't nothing about "feels like minus 14" that looks good on me. I promise not to complain too much about the weather, but today is the exception.

Yesterday, I hit up my local sporting goods store for some new winter gear. (I am so over freezing my a** off.) And truth be told, I've been running in the same few outfits for over a year.

Which means my shopping spree was completely warranted, right?

I was *thrilled* with my purchases:

- New long underwear. Finally.

- New gloves. (Or snot rags, however you look at it.)

- A few new Under Armour shirts.

- Lounge wear. (For sitting by the fire nursing my aching muscles.)

With my new gear in check, I thought I'd be ready for whatever Mother Nature threw my way today. Not freakin' so.

This was the first run in history where my butt cheeks got cold. (TMI, but true.) I was totally miffed at a few select name brands for marketing gear that doesn't get the f*ing job done.

When I got home, (4 miles today), I checked Weather.com. That's where I read 4 degrees. Feels like -14. Oh f*.

In that moment, I forgave Reebok, Under Armour and Adidas for their failings because I don't think there is a brand on the *planet* that could have kept me warm today.

Midas does NOT have a thyroid problem. Apparently, it's a mama error. So, he's back on the "no table scraps" diet. Sh*t.

I think I've said this before, but I'm no foodie.

Last night, Hubs and I found ourselves in a swanky cooking class on the rich side of town. We thought it would be something fun to do together. I'm sure he's thinking, "I'll do damn near anything to have my wife cook one good meal, even if it means I have to wear an apron, too."

If there were cooking skills to be inherited in my family, my brother most certainly got all of them. They bypassed me entirely.

Honestly though, I'm very thankful I don't love food. It's easy to cook because I don't. It's easy to shop because I never reference recipes. And it's easy to *eat* because my palate is simple.

I have spent my entire *life* having an affair with Cheerios, Cheetos and pasta, which I can assure you, does NOT bode well for marathon training.

For the last few months, I've really been struggling with nutrition.

It's a totally foreign concept to *fuel* my body vs. stuff my face. And honestly, I haven't, yet, fully embraced this ideology.

No one told me my addiction to cinnamon rolls and Mexican food would be my demise. I was under some sort of colourful impression I'd be able to eat whatever the hell I wanted with very little regard to fat, calories or sugar. Yeah, right.

So back to cooking class. That's why Hubs and I signed up. So I could build up my kitchen-goddess muscles. (The recipes they gave us were simple – thank you, Jesus.)

Every single day I find myself recommitting to nutrition. If I eat a cinnamon roll for lunch, I eat a hard-boiled egg and avocado for dinner. If I eat a half-a-bag of puff Cheetos (like I did this week), I tell myself there is no better time to do it than now.

I checked the weather before I left the house this morning. It was 24 degrees. A freakin' heat wave, so Midas and I put up 4 miles. My Caterpillar stocking hat is getting a workout.

A Life Worth Loving

A few years ago, I set up a magical P.O. Box.

I say magical because no one I owe money to knows about it. Only my VIPs. I never know what I'll find inside, but it's always something good.

Yesterday was no exception.

Inside was a small white box loaded with CDs from a good friend and a big fan of my marathon journey. The second package, a thin white envelope, held a small piece of art courtesy of a former client.

In colorful words, the art boldly declared: Make Your Life Worth Loving.

It stopped me in my tracks.

First, I had to take a picture. But second, I paused to consider my life. (Which is a weird a** thing to do at the post office, to be sure.)

In that moment, I thought to myself, "Is my life worth *loving*?" For a long time, the answer was probably not because there are a whole lot of "have to's." And not very many "get to's."

That said, I consider my marathon adventure a "get to" because the joy I feel every single day in sharing my experience completely blisses me out.

I don't think it's a coincidence I received these items yesterday.

It was a strong reminder to: Be grateful. Stay present. Set your life up the way you want to. Leap off a cliff. Go balls out. Love every single second, as best you can, of the time you have on the planet.

I'm in. How about you?

When I got home this morning, (a 2.5 mile leisurely walk), I threw away my Cheetos, cinnamon rolls and pita chips. If I want to live my best life, I'd better start acting like it.

Channeling Ms. Stewart

I channeled Martha Stewart in my kitchen last night.

I kept waiting for someone else to sweep in and "handle" my nutritional woes, but that's kind of like expecting someone else to run your miles. It never works. So, I finally decided to fix it.

Yesterday afternoon, I hit up the local grocery store for provisions. A mere $200 and 8 pounds of chicken later, I was on my way.

Here's what I cooked up: Chicken with Spring Veggies, Santa Fe Chicken Soup, Chicken with Parsley Orzo, Chicken Salad, Protein Bars and Fruit & Nut Bars.

You likely won't find me in the kitchen again for at least a year because cooking is an a** load of work. But dinner last night was fabulous and it ran circles around Cheerios.

Which leads me to this morning: It's been so bloody cold outside that the sage in me decided to hop up on the treadmill. Midas wasn't happy, but my extremities sure were.

Admittedly, the treadmill has its place and it's much easier on your joints. But the road warrior in me would take the cold, wind, rain or extreme heat over banging it out in the basement, any day.

Tomorrow I'm up for 12 miles and D.R. is on deck and ready to roll.

Right now I'm doing my best not to get bored running the same distances every week. The maniac in me is ready to push harder. Go farther. Get this f*ing show on the road.

Just remind me I said this in a few weeks when I'm scheduled for my first 16er.

I've been researching demographic information on marathoners. Only .5 percent of the U.S. population has ever run a marathon. The fastest marathon ever run was in 2:03:23. (Holy cripes – it wasn't me.) To put this in perspective, that's how long it takes me to run a half-marathon. On a good day.

Rolling With the Punches

Things don't always go my way.

I'm not one who usually complains, but today was one of those terrible-horrible-no-good-very-bad-long-run-days.

I have never really talked about what can go wrong on the road because truthfully, not a lot does. But, *today* happened to be the exception.

I flew out of bed ready to take on whatever came my way. Mentally, I was in the game. Hell, this morning I thought I owned the game.

I brushed my chicklets, threw on my gear, grabbed a cup o' joe and my headlamp, and headed out for my weekly long run.

The thermostat in my car read 40 degrees. I was giddy. I couldn't believe my good fortune. By the time I hit the trail head, it was 28. No problem. I had four layers on top, two on the bottom and D.R. just three short miles away.

I gave mittens a try on the first leg. Um, yeah. Not for me. They kept my fingers warm but limited my access to everything else. You won't find me wearing those chunky mounds of cotton ever again.

For some reason, (and only someone much smarter than me would know this), the temperature began to climb uber fast.

I was seriously drenched in sweat by mile two. I was hot. Irritated. Thirsty. My Under Armour shirt took on a life of its own. The situation was heading towards disaster. At that point, my only goal was to get to D.R.

But first, I had to conquer an unanticipated one-mile detour.

Listen. A 1-mile detour may be inconsequential to a cyclist, but it matters deeply to me and my dawgs.

By the grace of God, I made it to D.R.

I tore off half my clothes, chugged a gallon of water, ditched the mittens and headed back out to the trail.

Here were a few other hard-earned lessons today:

- Sometimes, your body isn't kidding. It has to pee.

- There are times when being a girl just plain sucks. (You'll have to read between the lines here.)

- Layering Under Armour shirts is a bad f*ing idea. At one point I was positive I had on a midriff. I don't care what anyone says, that is *not* hot.

- My ear buds tried to strangle me. I f*ed with those pesky pieces of plastic every 30 seconds for two-and-a-half hours. A terrible distraction.

- Try to account for detours and construction. Today, I was up for 12 and ended just over 14. Mentally, I wasn't prepared for 14. The last mile and a half my mantra was, "Do what's yours to do. Do what yours to do. Don't walk. Don't quit. Do what's your to do."

D.R. was a bright shining beacon of hope this morning.

I was able to ditch gear, switch gloves, chug water, hand off the water belt, chuckle, and shout out a few strong woot woots. At one point, she held a sign for me that read:

Who can do this thing? You can. You are amazing. You rock. You are strong. You don't quit. You can do this and more!

At the same time she hollered, "Who can do this? You can. Who can do this? You can."

And in that moment, I kept going.

Because someone else believed I could.

All in all, I can't complain about squeaking out 14 miles. (Albeit unintended.) You can bet you're a** I'll watch for detours next time.

Sole Sisters

I spent last night in my old stomping grounds.

That would be Casper, Wyoming, a town located approximately in the middle of nowhere. The cool thing about Wyoming is you never know who you're going to meet.

I ran up for a friend's birthday party, and ended up shaking hands with a woman who has run 15 marathons. Holy Cripes.

Her goal? Two per year.

Honestly, I would never compare my journey to her heroic accomplishments. But, after hearing her story, I realized:

1) Anything IS possible; and

2) I don't have a single complaining leg to stand on.

It seems like I hem, haw and moan about everything these days. Shin splints. Binge eating. Gear that tries to strangle me. The cold. Layers. Detours. (You catch my drift?)

I guess when you've run 15 marathons you have your sh*t down to a science.

While chatting up the birthday girl, I learned she and a few of her girlfriends are running the half marathon of the same race I'm running my first full.

Sometimes, the world is a small, small place.

My sole-sister radar has become undeniably stronger. Everywhere I go, I connect with other runners. Women who love the road. Love to run.

Women who are laying it all on the line for their health, to reach a goal, to prove they can, or for the simple joy of doing it.

I'm honored to be among them.

After yesterday's long run disaster, :I took this morning off. F it.*

$50 Socks

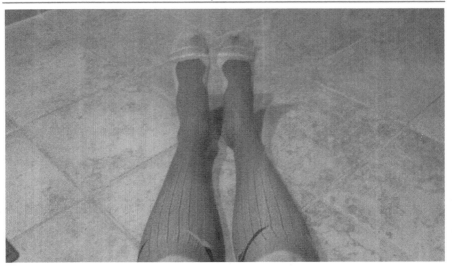

I ordered my first ever pair of compression socks.

The price tag on these suckers is $50 bucks a pair. Thankfully, I picked up two pair on sale for $60.

I used to think compression socks were for people with diabetes or for those who just had open-heart surgery. I was wrong. But hell, I've been wrong about a lot of things.

I gave 'em a go this morning. I was a little worried because these socks look freakin' tiny. And my dawgs were thinking, "No way, man. We're not squeezing into those." (They're still a bit peeved from our run on Saturday.)

It took four minutes to get them on, up and situated - I'm not kidding when I say they're f*ing tight.

But ohhhhhhlaaaaaaalaaaaaa... they are fantabulous.

Here's what Yahoo says: "They provide the perfect level of compression to energize your limbs before, during and after all athletic activities. These products will help to enhance your athletic performance."

I don't know if they enhanced my performance this morning, (four miles), but shockingly, my limbs did feel energized. I wouldn't go so far as to say I was running on sunshine. But there was a noticeable difference.

I wondered if they had whole body compression mechanisms. But, my organs would probably collapse under the pressure. Not cool. And if it took me 17 minutes to peel *off* the socks, an entire body suit might chew up a day.

Thank you for letting me complain my head off after Saturday's long run. I had an outpouring of emails – and phone calls – from people asking if I was okay. You rock.

Full On Bat Sh*t

In my world, 4:30 a.m. is the perfect time to run.

You rarely see other peeps. Midas and I have the road mostly to ourselves. There's no drama, mishaps or dog wars to diffuse.

But lately, I've been sleeping like a mofo, which is another way to say I'm having a hell of a time getting out of bed. Between work and training, I require a full 8 hours every night to even halfway function the next day.

This week, I gave myself permission to sleep in. Which means Midas and I were off our normal time by about 45 minutes; today, we paid dearly for it.

God bless. There were dogs *everywhere*. And in my world, that's a recipe for disaster. Other Dogs + Midas = Sh*t Storm.

Now, don't kid yourself. I love my dog like a child. But there are days he's a total a**hole. He would love to eat, (or eliminate), every other dog in the neighborhood.

When he sees a dog out in its yard, he freaks out. When he sees another dog run past our yard, he comes *unhinged*.

But, the very worst is when we have to run by another dog that is on a leash, with its owner, on the *other* side of the street.

He goes full-on *bat sh*t*.

I must have missed the memo requesting every single person in my neighborhood, (with a dog), be out between 5:30 a.m. and 6:20 a.m. this morning.

I half ran and was half dragged in every direction imaginable. My leash-carrying arm is damn lucky to still be in the socket. I think I left some tread (or skin!) on the side of the road.

Today's lesson for me is this: "Sister, if you want to avoid drama, keep your arm in its socket and have a peaceful morning run, get your freakin' a** out of bed before the rooster crows."

A Mission To Save The Girls

When God was handing out boobs, I got the short end of the stick.

I'm not complaining; he gave me lots of other "friendly" qualities to make up for it. But what I *do* have, I'm on a mission to protect.

Last year, when I ran my first 10k, my girlfriend encouraged me to download MapMyRun to my phone. (It tracks your calories, miles, incline, pace, etc.) So I did.

And then I proceeded to gently place my phone "between my girls" and off I went.

It worked. I was hooked.

Every week, when I'd head out for my long run, I'd start the app, tuck the phone in my sports bra and hit the trail. Things went on like this for six to eight weeks. And then, if finally happened:

I fried my phone with sweat.

If you've ever stepped foot into a Verizon store, you know why this sucks. Long lines. Outrageous wait times and $400 phones.

With one phone down, I reached out to my Facebook friends looking for answers.

Their No.1 solution?

Put your phone in a Ziploc bag *before* you put it between your boobs.

So here we are six months later, and I am still on the Ziploc plan. The problem with using a Ziploc is that it chews the ever lovin' sh*t out of your chest. And that's putting it mildly.

Think cat going crazy in the middle of the night, scratches everywhere. You don't know how freakin' pointy the corners of that little plastic bag really are 'til you put one somewhere it was never meant to be.

So I asked my brilliant Facebook friends, again, for a workable solution.

An arm band.

Who knew the answer could be so simple?

So I perused Amazon for a gadget that would fit my phone. (And my monster pipes.)

I had to measure my bicep just to make sure it wasn't too small. Mine bust out of the measuring tape at 10.5 inches. I know, a show stopper.

Today, my new arm band arrives in the mail, and I'm going to do everything in my power to make it work.

Because my girls are depending on me.

It's snowy and cold here today so I ran 3.15 miles on the treadmill. Midas was p*ssed, but he'll survive.

13,260 Days And Counting

Yesterday I hit up my favorite running store.

My preferred choice happens to be Boulder Running Company. I really like their people. I dig their service, and I appreciate their insights, wisdom and knowledge about gear and running.

Collette was assigned to help me find the perfect pair of shoes. She's a marathoner seven times over; and she happens to be the same sales clerk who told me months ago, (when I bought my last pair of shoes), that I'd have to give something up if I decided to train for a marathon.

At the time I didn't believe her.

Yesterday, I got the chance to tell her she was right. And I thanked her.

For giving it to me straight and for making me eat crow.

I spent 90 minutes trying on shoes. (That's the diva in me.)

A mere $250 later, I walked out with a new pair of Brooks, the perfect jacket, (for my long, blustery morning runs), and lots and lots of sports chews.

Now, more than ever, I'm following the magic of this journey. I'm honoring my intuition about what's mine to do, my next steps, everything.

After my shopping spree, I hoofed it to Barnes & Noble. I was led to this book: *20,000 Days and Counting* by Robert D. Smith. It's a true story about a guy who woke up one day and realized he'd been alive for 20,000 days.

So he promptly checked himself into a hotel and spent 48 hours planning his next 20,000 days.

Today, (not counting leap years or whatever), I've been on this planet for 13,260 days.

And I can say with complete authority there is *nothing* I'd rather do than start my next 13,260 days doing *this*.

The Mile-7 Curse

It's happened before on a 14-mile run, so I should have been prepared.

Today, I pulled the plug at mile seven.

Part of me is pretty damn upset because long runs matter. And part of me is super proud that I actually listened to my body. (A first, I swear.)

This morning started like every other long run.

D.R. and I hooked up at the church and off I went. Smooth sailing, baby.

It started to get messy around mile six: a dreaded side cramp.

Hey, I'm no wuss. I run in 14-degree weather. I rarely miss a day of training. I'm talking a side cramp that feels like you're having appendicitis. (Not that I know what that feels like, as I still have my appendix, but it's got to be close.)

I told myself to breathe through it. Run around it. I even begged God to magically dissolve it. And each of these tactics worked for about 20 seconds.

At mile 7, I knew I was finished.

Last year, two weeks before my first half-marathon, I bought new shoes.

They were beautiful, well designed and they carried MY name. (Brooks.) I loved them.

On race day, a half-mile before the finish line, I thought I was having appendicitis. (Sound familiar?) Thankfully it wasn't, but I knew something was very, very wrong.

The next week, when I attempted my first 14er, the same thing happened at mile 7. I walked the whole f*ing way back to the car. (No joke.)

I complained to my chiropractor about a side cramp. He said, "Tell me about your shoes." I exclaimed, "Oh, it can't be my shoes; they're brand new." He came back with, "Exactly."

So, I pulled the old tried-and-trues from retirement. No further cramping.

I share this story because today I ran in my new treads. They're beautiful, well designed and carry MY name.

I can't tell you for certain the shoes were to blame.

But, what I can say is that my ASICS will be back on my dawgs next week for the BIG 1-6.

Here are my other lessons:

- I am buying wireless ear buds for my Shuffle today. I can't be bothered with that sh*t one more Saturday.

- Hands down, a support person is the best investment I have made. Today, D.R. drove me back to my car. Hence, I didn't have to walk or call a cab. A total, unexpected blessing.

- I'll be sticking to ASICS for the rest of my marathon training. No exceptions. The new treads will go in the "cute with jeans" collection.

I had self-defense class last night – freakin' awesome! Read on for deets.

My Own Brand of Whoop A**

I spent Friday night learning all kinds of bad a** moves.

As it was my first-ever self-defense class, I had no idea what to expect or what I'd learn. It was anybody's guess if I'd love it, hate it or run out the front door crying.

It's scary to think about scary sh*t. So most of us don't. That said, safety has been top-of-mind for the last few weeks. Why? Because not too long ago, a woman was sexually assaulted on a trail close to where I live.

That led to a few changes in my training protocol:

- I hired a support person. (Who also has her concealed weapons permit.)

- I now carry mace on the first leg of every long run. (It's dark!)

- I signed up for and successfully completed a self-defense class.

The class was ridiculously good. I learned about awareness. Boundaries. Conflict. How to use my adrenaline and my voice. I also got some kick-a** moves.

I now have tools for:

1. Handling an uncomfortable verbal confrontation.

2. How to fight my way out of an attack from the front.

3. Opening a can of BK whoop a** if I'm blindsided from the back.

The class gave me permission to stand up for myself. Say no. Be a full-on b*tch if need be.

As women, we are programmed to be nice. Most of the time, we have no boundaries because we're taught at a young age to "go along to get along." Not anymore.

You f* with me, I will bring on the stink.

I will go after your eyes. I will knee you in the privates. I will elbow you in the face. And that's just the beginning.

The truth is, I can only hope I'll never need to use any of what I learned.

But hope is not a strategy. Being prepared is.

Midas and I trekked through several inches of snow this morning. We did some shovelling in lieu of weights.

Bathroom Business

One of my girlfriends e-mailed me recently.

She had a story to share about being in the mountains on a six-mile trek with her pooch. At the farthest point from her car, her stomach started to gurgle.

Not the "I'm-just-hungry" gurgle.

The "I-think-I-might-sh*t-my-pants" gurgle.

"What to do?" she lamented.

If she ran, it would likely come out. If she walked, it would take her forever to get to the car.

I honestly don't know how the story ended. (I think she made it to the car.) But the point of her email was, "Brook, how do you handle bathroom business while training?" It's the No. 1 thing people ask me when they learn I'm training for a marathon.

Here's the truth: My short runs are no big deal. So far, neither are my long runs. But, I'm running in the dead of winter. In Denver. *Outside.* Guess how many port-a-potties and/or bathrooms are open along the trail right now. ZERO. And they don't open until April. (One month *before* the marathon.)

D.R. and I were discussing this very topic last week. Here's what she's thinking: *"I thought about configuring a hula-hoop drape you could step into. I could pull it up and hold it while you pull down your drawers, pee and take off again in a flash. No stopping in a restaurant or gas station. We have to streamline this thing like it's the Indy 500."*

I laughed out loud for an entire freakin' day. First off, I don't run at a speed that warrants being compared to the Indy. But, I think she may be on to something. I'm not sure where we will shake out, but if D.R. does build a "pee machine," I will most definitely share the deets with you.

It snowed over 12 inches here yesterday, so I was back on the treadmill for 5.2 miles this morning. The miles will start cranking up next week. I'd best be ready.

Learning to Let Sh*t Go

When I run on the treadmill, I hide the dashboard.

It seems like 30 minutes takes forever. That it's heroic just to burn your first 100 calories. I try to tell myself the numbers aren't important; that I should just run until the machine turns off.

Today, I peeked behind the towel at 29 minutes and 41 minutes. And I tore the towel clean off at 47 minutes so I knew *exactly* how much time I had left.

Truthfully, I am a highly structured person. I like to know exactly where I am, what I'm doing and where I'm going. So it's a big challenge for me to take my hands off the wheel of anything in my life. (Think relationships, my business, marathon training – everything.)

But, a huge part of this adventure is letting sh*t go, trusting I'll have what I need. Trusting that the answers will come. Amazingly enough, they always do.

Yesterday, I chatted up my old personal trainer. Shari started me off on the right foot a few years ago with some very effective weight training. On the call, I complained about how tired I've been, and that I struggle with fatigue and hunger around 11 a.m. (The story of my freakin' life these days.)

She asked what I was eating for breakfast. I boasted about my "meaty" smoothies lovingly put together in my Vita Mix blender.

She said, "Your blood sugar is crashing, likely because of all the fruit you're eating. Try to incorporate more fat and protein. Ease up on the fruit and add a few more veggies." She also recommended flax seed and almond butter.

Today, I skipped the smoothie and opted for oatmeal with almond butter and blueberries. I won't know until 11 a.m. if this is a better plan. But I trust Shari. And I'm learning to trust I will have exactly what I need when I need it.

It's snowing like crazy here, so 5.2 miles on the treadmill this morning. I would have stopped at three miles if I didn't have to report to you.

I Could Not Have Known

I sleep with my phone next to my bed.

The first thing I do when I wake up every morning is lean over and check my e-mail. (It's a nasty habit.) I do it before I even have the chance to offer up thanks for being given another day to "get things right." (I hate to admit this, but, unfortunately, it's true.)

This morning, I had a fabulous email waiting for me from someone I've never met. Here's a glimpse of what she wrote:

"I have several friends who are running in a 5k race in Raleigh, N.C., Charlotte, N.C., and the Outer Banks. I came across your site by chance, and I'm happy I did. Do you think I would be ready? If I can't run it, I will walk it. I want this! I want to be healthy! I want to begin the work toward wellness and good health."

And yesterday, a fellow sole sister, (also someone I've never met), left this on the blog:

"Hi! I wanted to send you some encouragement! Your story is much like mine. I never had run in my life until January 2012. I decided I would try it. I ran my first 5k in March, a half-marathon in October, a 10k in November and then a full marathon 2 weeks ago! It took me 4 hours, 42 minutes. Best time of my life! Good luck in your training. I'm rooting for you!"

Then, on Facebook, another note:

"I think this is just a plain awesome site – love reading your blogs – the true challenges of running, staying motivated. One of the most real blogs about working out and running I have ever read. Thank you for sharing and always looking forward to seeing more."

Listen. I'm no superstar. I'm a girl with a dream. (And an outrageously big goal.)

I struggle. Fall down. Get discouraged. Fight my way back. Bake cinnamon rolls. Throw them away. Blow out, bail on a run, down a half-a-bag-of Cheetos and turn around and do everything in my power to come back stronger.

Hands down, the best thing about this journey is my community: the peeps who cheer for, believe in and support me. The people who want to do this with me, and who want to do something totally awesome for *themselves*.

Every note, every word of encouragement, matters.

It was just a few weeks ago that I sat in a hotel room and got the silly idea to blog about training for my first marathon. And every day since, I've done my best to share the honest-to-God truth about what it really takes.

I could not have known then what I know now. That having support can make or break you. I could never have imagined that giving others behind-the-scenes, VIP access to my journey would fuel me and keep me moving.

So, I'm all in for the next 80+ days, and I'm thrilled beyond belief that you're with me.

I'm going out to dinner tonight. My plan is to throw down on a ridiculously big piece of red meat. Hey, I'm a girl from Nebraska. If you don't eat red meat, they damn near disown you.

FREE RESOURCE: If you're ready to join a community of other powerful, amazing sole sisters, come on over and say hey at www.Facebook.com/BrooksFirstMarathon. I can't wait to meet you!

March Worries Me Most

I'm not very sophisticated in my record keeping.

But, at least I'm consistent.

Each day, I sit down and record my miles in a paper journal. Every run, walk, hike and bike ride. It's an important ritual for me.

I started logging each activity because someone once said I'd run between 300 to 500 miles to train for a marathon, which means I could have run from Denver to St. Louis by the time I'm done. What the hell.

I'll end up on the high side because that's just how I roll. I also want to know I did every last thing in my power to reach my goal, without having to crawl (or limp!) across the finish line.

February was a crazy. Lots of days with sub-freezing temperatures. A complete blow-out on a long run. Too much snow in the mountains to hike.

All that said, here's where things shook out:

February	Total-To-Date
Ran: 122.59 miles	Running: 238.59 miles
Walked: 30.01 miles	Walking: 56.01 miles
Hiked: 4 miles	Hiking: 8 miles
Biked: ZERO	Biking: 24.5
Midas Total: 95.74 R/W/H	Midas T-T-D: 152.24

I look at Midas's numbers and have a hard time believing he's overweight. I look at *my* numbers and it's crystal clear why I can eat a house.

When I worked out my training calendar, the month I worried about most was March. My long run schedule is 16, 10, 18, 12, 18.

OH f*. That's 74 miles, just on Saturdays.

If I can make it through March without incident or injury, I know I'll make it to race day. I actually know I will anyway, but that doesn't make what lies ahead any freakin' easier.

I jokingly told someone I am running into March an amateur. God willing, I will run out the other side a PRO.

Oh, hell yes, I did eat a big fat piece of red meat last night. It's the first time in a month I felt full. The boys back home would be proud.

Uber Low Tolerance

I got my hair cut yesterday.

Thank God; it was long overdue. And you know how bad it feels when you need a haircut? It tilts my world. A few weeks ago I mentioned I might go el natural. Yeah, um. No way.

My gal has been cutting my hair for the past five years. She's a total rock star. Not only is she one of the best "make-me-beautiful" people I've ever met, but she is a cross-fit super hero. She plays in a rock band. She loves tattoos. She's a great Mom. And she gives back to her community.

I loved her the moment I met her.

Here's why:

She is who she is. Seriously, you can love her or leave her; it's no skin off her nose. She's one of the most authentic people I know. She has amazing clarity about who she is and how she shows up in the world.

And her tolerance for bull sh*t is pretty f*ing low.

Mine too.

If you want to talk about the price of gas or the weather, these days I'm not your girl. If you want to make small talk, keep *moving*.

But if you want to throw down, get in the trenches, be real, live passionately, or plain "get loud" about life, I'm in.

I'm rounding the corner on the half-way point of training, which means I still have a long ways to go. But I'm starting to shed the sh*t that doesn't work, (extra pounds, bad habits, life situations), and embrace what does.

I knew training for a marathon would be the physical challenge of a lifetime. But I had no idea how much it would change me spiritually, emotionally and mentally, too.

I like the person I'm becoming.

Tomorrow is my first 16-er. Prayers welcome.

A Lot To Prove

Day 43

I laid down my first ever 16-mile run today.

It wasn't pretty. But it was honest. I had a lot to prove to myself today:

- That I was mentally prepared.

- That I was right about my shoes.

- That I am meant to run a marathon.

- That I could lay down a new personal best.

We got 'er done.

I've had a rough go the last two weeks. A construction detour and a side cramp nearly wrecked me. Last night, while pulling together my gear, I had a total meltdown.

Who am I to do this? What if I can't? What if I don't? Will my shoes take me there? Will my legs? Am I out of my f*ing mind to even do this?

I reached out to a few friends who were more than willing to lend some inspiration. My good friend Jack was brazen enough to tell me Ryan

Gosling would be waiting at the finish line. (It turned out to be a bold lie, but WTF; it worked.)

Today, I went back to basics, which means I pulled out all of the reliable tools that got me this far in the first place.

- Experienced treads. (Shoes)

- Ancient long-underwear. (Folks, this sh*t is ratty -- we're talking 15-years old.)

- My broken down Adidas socks. (The pair with two holes from a dog bite a few months ago. Seriously, who gets bitten by a three-pound dog and talks about it?)

- I said hell to the NO to my Under Armour Shirts. (Someone told me the midriff was out. Thank God.)

- And I duct taped my ear buds to my chest.

In case you think I'm kidding, I'm not. I tore off a one-inch piece and planted it firmly over the wire. It helps eliminate the drag effect – you know, when your buds are stretched too tight and you're worried they'll fall out of your ears.

As far as long runs go, today was about as good as it gets. Sure, a few things weren't perfect, but I was damn thankful just to be doing this.

When the sun was in my eyes at mile five, I told myself, "It's all good sister. It means you're still running." When I got a hitch in my side at mile 13, I told myself, "It doesn't feel like appendicitis. Keep truckin'." When my brain lost contact with my legs at mile 14, I was thankful they knew what to do on their own. And when Beyoncé brought me down the home stretch with her song "Naughty Girl" I felt myself shift from survivor to total bad a**.

I'll be honest. This morning my confidence was shaky at best. But, I came out on the other side re-committed to killing the rest of my training schedule and BECOMING a marathoner.

D.R. was a Super Star again today. I am blessed.

The $1K Club

I want to let you in on a secret.

I've done a ton of behind-the-scenes work to set myself up for success training for this marathon: I started a blog, created a FB Page, asked a good friend, Father English, to create a customized prayer for me, hired D.R. and formed the $1K Club with my sister-in-law Dannika.

Dannika had her second baby last October. (On my birthday, no less.) Around Christmas, she was complaining about the baby weight. She said she'd like to lose a few pounds and get back into her skinny jeans.

So I challenged her: "Put your money where your mouth is, sister. Mail me a check for $1,000 and I'll hold you accountable to reaching your goal weight by June 30."

She laughed. (She thought I was joking. If you know me, you know I never joke about sh*t like this.) Then, she asked, "Well, what would I hold you accountable for? You don't have any weight to lose."

I said, "I'll run a marathon before June 30." (I'm such a dumb a**.)

So the deal was struck, and we promptly went on the hunt for a few other fools who wanted to play in our sand box. We had four other takers, which means there is $6,000 up for grabs. If you reach your goal, you get your check back. If you don't, it gets cashed and the winners split the money.

I really don't want to cash anyone's check. I don't want my check cashed either. I'd much rather see each of us reach our goal. Because there's something very powerful about a group of women who are willing to shut up, put up and step up to get healthy, stay motivated and achieve greatness.

I woke up this morning and my legs were freakin' cryin'. Not just a slight ache, but a HolyCripesAlmightyIMayNeverWalkAgain ache. So, I did the only think I know to do. Midas and I ran three miles. Surprisingly, I feel better.

FREE RESOURCE: Want to start your own $1K Club? Get the full details at www.MarathonTrainingTools.com.

Expensive Doesn't Always Equal Best

I've spared no expense training for this marathon.

In fact, I'm keeping a running total of just how much money I'm spending, from start to finish, to put this beast to bed on my terms. My expenses to date include:

- Gloves
- Shoes
- Jacket
- Support Person

- Entry Fee
- Chiropractic Care
- Massage
- Pedicures

I think I'll end up somewhere between $2,000 to $3,000, but I still have 70-plus days to go so it's anybody's guess.

Here's a very important lesson I've learned: Expensive doesn't always equal best.

My long run on Saturday was perfect. When I got home and peeled off all my layers, I noticed the magnets in my new jacket left a hickey on my neck. It took me a full day to figure out what caused the irritation. (I seriously thought it was the stress of 16 miles.)

That jacket cost me $150.

Same goes for my new shoes. I thought I'd be running on sunshine from now until May in my new treads. But after calling it quits at mile seven a couple weeks ago, they went in the "cute with jeans" pile.

That mistake?

Another $150.

Then yesterday, Hubs and I went out for a death march on our bikes. We turned around at 3.5 miles because his tires didn't have enough air.

Another mistake. (Albeit a cheaper one.)

Here's the lesson:

I'm not a gear geek. Never have been. Never gave a rip. Until this marathon, I honestly paid very little attention to what I wore, what I ate, if I had the right gear, why it mattered, why you should think about sh*t before you do it, what you need, why some things work and some things simply don't.

All this sh*t matters.

I mentioned a few days ago that I went back to basics. And that's where I'm planning to stay. I may cross the finish line in a holey pair of long-underpants and a ratty ol' jacket.

But if that's what it takes, so be it.

Midas and I went out for four miles this morning. I can usually count on him to stop and pee at least a dozen times, (so I can catch my breath). Today, he stopped twice, which means the hills were killer.

Old As Sh*t, Young At Heart.

It was 12 degrees when Midas and I set out to rock the road this morning.

There is no other way to say it – that's f*ing cold.

I almost have my gear down to a science, but the one part of my body that is not fully covered during a run is my face. And I'm here to tell you, it takes a *beating*.

I was driving home from my long run on Saturday and flipped the visor down to keep the sun from my eyes. What I saw in the mirror wasn't good. My sunspots were raging. The skin around my mouth was peeling. I also had those white, slimy mouth boogers everywhere. My skin was in desperate need of exfoliation, sun spot killer and hydration.

Altitude, sun and cold, combined with a ridiculously fast pace of 6 mph, is a sure-fire way to add 10 years to your mug. And to that I say, "No freakin' way." I did some quick research on how altitude affects your skin. (Denver is the Mile High City after all…)

Here's what I found:

- Altitude drastically increases risk of sunburn, premature aging, and melanomas due to the stronger presence of UV rays and free radicals in the thinned atmosphere.

- Because the air is usually totally devoid of any form of moisture, there is a significantly higher risk of experiencing dry, irritated skin, facial redness, and eczema.

No kidding.

On the flip side, the Washing Times said Denver is ranked Top 10 for helping its residents stay young.

The only conclusion I can draw is that we all look old as sh*t but we're young at heart.

Right now I use a daily exfoliant, sun spot remover, coconut oil and sunscreen on my face. It's probably not what Angelina Jolie uses, but she's not training for a marathon.

One of Many Gifts

I'm a big believer in signs.

You know, like from God. The Universe. Whatever Higher Power works for you. And I believe other people are often the messengers.

A few months ago I was flying home from the east coast and ended up sitting next to a funny, brilliant man from Florida. He had no intention of letting me sleep on the plane. (Think super chatty, which is weird for a guy.)

We discussed love, marriage, books, protein bars, Vita Mix blenders, the works. We got to the "heart" of the matter on a number of topics uber quick. (It's amazing what you'll tell a stranger because you'll never see them again.)

He recommended I read *The Mastery of Love*, by Don Miguel Ruiz.

Being a believer in signs, I did.

Here's a quick excerpt – and I'm paraphrasing just a bit:

So many humans are suffering because of all the false images we try to project. Humans pretend to be something very important, but at the same time, we believe we are nothing. We work so hard to be someone, to be recognized and approved by others… to be powerful, rich, to be famous.

My interpretation is we all run around hoping others will perceive us one way, but the truth of who we are is someone entirely different.

How exhausting. (And boring!)

I share all this because today, my professional and personal worlds collided. I gave my business peeps a behind the scenes look at what's up in my personal life. (I shared my blog, the Brook's First Marathon Face Book page and my marathon journey.)

My entire life I've worked really f*ing hard to keep my professional life separate from who I am spiritually, energetically, emotionally and personally.

And it worked for a long, long time.

But it doesn't work anymore.

It doesn't work because I can't stand it. I refuse to separate who I am in hopes of winning someone over. We're each born with a unique set of gifts and talents. And it would be a damn shame to sit quietly and watch the life we're supposed to live pass us by.

That's one of the many gifts in training for a marathon.

Now everyone I know will know I'm a cusser, that I binge on sugar cookies, that I fall down all over the freakin' place and do everything in my power to pull my sh*t together and come back stronger.

But, they'll also see I'm a person of my word. When I say I'm going to do something, I'll pull out all the stops to make it happen.

They'll know I'm a girl who strives to shine every single day so others are empowered to do the same.

What a gift.

Midas and I put up four miles this morning. It's a heat wave over here with temperatures in the low 20s.

Extraterrestrial Alert

Around the first of the year, I went to see a psychic.

I won't go in to all of the details, but somehow the fact that I run outside in the wee hours of the morning made its way into our conversation.

She asked where I lived. I told her.

She said, "There are extraterrestrials out in your area between 3:30 a.m. – 5:00 a.m. You haven't seen them because you aren't open to seeing them."

So every morning for the last few months I've been on E.T. alert. (I'm so not kidding.)

This morning, it crossed my mind she might be right.

Midas and I headed out at 4:50 a.m. Same ol' same ol'. At the bottom of the first hill, he stopped to point. (Midas has no formal training, so when he cocks his leg in the air, something's up.)

I pulled my ear buds out to listen. It sounded like a mountain lion eating a baby. (Whatever the freak that sounds like…)

Cacaw! Cacaw! Screech, Screech, Cacaw! Cacaw!

Midas refused to budge for a full 30 seconds. And I thought to myself, "Well self, this might just be the morning we get eaten."

After 30 seconds, I put my buds back in, yanked on the leash and off we went. At the farthest point from the house, a deer came crashing out of the bushes.

Ten feet from my face.

I screamed. (Yes, out loud. I'm sure the neighbors were like, "You fruity b*tch. You flash your headlamp through my windows every morning and now this?!?!?)

I then proceeded to grab my chest, fall to the ground and roll around crying out for my life.

Okay, it wasn't that bad. But when I hollered out, Midas went bat sh*t, too.

As we pushed on I thought, "WTF? It feels like we're running through the Michael Jackson Thriller video this morning. Awesome way to start the day."

On the home stretch, I look over to see a dozen pair of glassy eyes staring back at us. For a split second I thought, "It's finally happening. I'm seeing the extraterrestrials." But a closer look revealed it was a family of deer lounging in my neighbor's front yard.

I realized today that daylight saving time is Sunday, which means we will continue to run in the dark for a few more weeks.

But I'm a watchin'. And I carry a stealthy, secret camera.

If I happen to cross paths or throw down with an E.T., you'll be the first to know.

We put up four miles again today. I read that as you approach your marathon you should be running 40-50 miles per week. Who f*ing does that?

Never Discount Your Miles

D.R. unveiled my custom-made pee-machine today.

It's a hula-hoop, a few safety pins and some high-end decorator fabric. And while I totally love it, thank God today I didn't need to *use* it.

My long run was moved up because we're expecting 14 inches of snow tomorrow. I planned to go it alone. (D.R. has a full-time job, so I was pretty sure she was out.)

Here's what's crazy: Not having her close worried me. I am used to the idea that she's "there" every two to four miles to make sure I make it to the next rendezvous point. Post-marathon, I may face some heavy duty co-dependency issues.

As luck would have it, she was able to meet. We did the water bottle hand-off and away I went. My plan was to run 12 miles. Instead I opted for 13.4.

As always, here are my lessons:

    1)   There will always be something a little scary on a long run.

A side cramp. A homeless man under a bridge. A group of young men in black sweatshirts smoking cigarettes. Cyclists whizzing by from behind. There's really no choice: Run through it and do your best to be "ready" for anything.

2) McDonald's and IHOP will be successful until the end of time because their sh*t smells so good.

Every long run I endure the aroma of fresh baked bread, maple syrup, hash browns and whatever else they're whipping up for their customers. While I would never stop, don't kid yourself, my taste buds are always cryin'.

3) Never discount your miles.

Next week will be my first 18-er. So it's easy to tell myself, "Oh, 10 miles? You should be able to do THAT in your sleep. 13 miles? Who cares! You're only half way to a marathon."

The truth is, putting up a double digit is never easy. I still sweat. I wonder if I'll finish. My legs get sore. Hell, sometimes they go numb. What I've learned is, no matter what the goal is for the week, take it seriously. Prepare. Show up 1,000 percent. Leave nothing to chance.

Approach every single long run like it matters. Because it does.

Tomorrow is the first Saturday in months that I don't have a long run scheduled. I told D.R. I plan to make chili and lay on my a** most of the day.

We'll see if I can sit still that long.

For The Record

I spent Friday night making delicious, healthy protein bars.

Truth be told, I also guzzled some homemade hooch.

The protein bar recipe came from a personal trainer; the hooch came from the storage room in my basement. Hubs and I are amateur wine makers; he makes the wine and I drink it.

While I was slaving away, my Mom called. We caught up on all of the world news from my hometown. She also shared the latest health tips from Dr. Oz.

When it was my turn, I chatted her head off about what's new in the world of marathon training. (Think extraterrestrials, my custom-made pee machine and laying down 13.4 miles yesterday.)

When I finished, she said something to the effect of, "This comes easy for you because you're passionate about exercise. Running. Fitness in general." And I thought, seriously? You're my mother. Do you not know me at all?

It's time to set the record straight: I am NOT passionate about running. I'm definitely not passionate about exercise. I mean seriously, if you could have perfect health, fit in to your skinny jeans, (effortlessly,) and run a marathon without training, wouldn't you choose that route instead?!

Here's what I am on fire about:

Living boldly. Setting a colossal goal and getting it done on my terms. Connecting with other people in an authentic, honest way. And proving to myself I can do anything I choose.

It turns out; this marathon is the conduit to having nearly everything I want in this life. Who knew?

All joking aside, thanks Mom, for everything. I love you.

Superstar Support Staff

I'd like you to meet Donna.

A.K.A. D.R. and teammate No. 2 for Brook's First Marathon. This woman is my raving fan… someone who will do damn near anything to make sure I cross the finish line in May, including:

- Create the world's first pee-machine.

- Custom-make signs to keep me inspired.

- Holler out chants and cheers so my legs keep movin'.

- Show up on a Friday (before she goes to work!) to make sure I complete my long run safely.

Every long run, she sees me at my absolute worst: No make-up. The infamous Caterpillar hat. Mouth boogers. Heavy breathing. Clothes that don't match. Lips that can barely form words because it's so freakin' cold outside. (And she hugs me anyway.)

She's never late. Never misses a rendezvous point. She's always standing by with a water bottle, my *other* gloves, an extra pair of shoes and some snacks. She is ready for whatever I might throw her way.

Some days, I don't need much. Others, I ditch clothes, hand off my water belt, ask for a snack and chug a half-gallon of water. Then she sends me on my way with a, "Who can do this? You can! Who can do this? You can!"

A few weeks ago, I posted a PT contract position on Craigslist to see if anyone on the planet would be willing to meet me at the a** crack of dawn every Saturday for 14 weeks.

I was looking for someone to haul water and carry extra gear and food, someone to meet me at pre-determined locations along the trail, someone to call the freakin' police if I went missing.

What I got was so much more: A cheerleader, a fan, a friend, a true teammate... and someone who is as committed to this journey as I am.

Today, I'm giving Donna some big love for who she is, for everything she does, for the laughs and stories she's provided.

And most importantly, I'd like to thank her for pulling out all the stops and for doing whatever it takes to guarantee I cross the finish line on race day.

D.R. – My most heartfelt thanks. God knew exactly what he was doing when he put us together. I am humbled, honored and grateful.

FREE RESOURCE: If you haven't yet downloaded the ad I ran on Craigslist for a part-time support person, go to www.MarathonTrainingTools.com.

Marathon Training Schedule

Midas and I are on the two-a-day program.

We have been for years. We usually exercise twice a day, once in the morning with a 3 to 5 mile run and once in the afternoon for a leisurely stroll.

Midas is a bit of a celebrity in our neighborhood. Many a neighbor walks down our driveway (daily!) just to say hello. People stop us on the hiking trail and call him by his first name. Others pull their car over, roll down their window and shout out, "Your dog is beautiful!"

More people know his name than know my name. If I didn't love him so much I'd be jealous. Most of our outings take place without incident. But I guaranfreakintee they're always filled with his personal brand of bat sh*t.

I share my two-a-day program because a lot of people have asked about my marathon-training schedule.

Honestly, I took a hybrid approach.

I did extensive research online and found dozens of different training plans. Some start from a zero-mile base. Others start from a 5k or 10k. A few were just for women, some were for people who prefer to walk one minute for every nine or ten they run.

I wanted a plan that progressed in miles on the weekend, but kept me somewhat level during the week. (I max out at 6 on a weekday, which is all I have time for in the mornings.)

I also wanted to log as many miles as possible before the big day.

I'm sharing my schedule for a couple reasons: So you'd know where I'm headed and hold me accountable and so you could decide if a marathon is something you'd like to add to your bucket list.

There has yet to be a day when I feel like I "have" to do this. Every day I fly out of bed excited that I get to.

FREE RESOURCE: You can view my training schedule at www.MarathonTrainingTools.com.

Eating On The Run

All of my extra brain space this week is being spent preparing for my 18-mile run.

I'm thinking about what to wear. (So I don't end up with a not-so-sexy midriff or chafing.) I'm mapping out my mental game. (I.e., how to break down the miles so I'm not overwhelmed.) I'm also kicking around how and what I'll eat on the run.

On my first 16-er a few weeks ago, I ran straight into hell at mile 14. So this week, I'm getting uber serious (and strategic!) about how I will fuel my body to lay down 18 miles without fainting, puking or dying.

Here's what my late-night research netted:

- Your body doesn't care if you eat carbs before you start your run.

- It does care about what you eat the night before. (And at what time.)

- You can run about 90 minutes without food with very little consequence.

The problem is, on an 18-mile run, I'll be out for more than three hours.

A basic rule of thumb, (according to peeps much smarter than me), is to take in 100 calories after an hour of running and then another 100 calories every 40 to 45 minutes. You can get your calories from solid foods or sport drinks, whichever you prefer.

Someone in an online forum recommended eating candy corn for an instant rush. I say no way. For starters, it tastes like sh*t. Not to mention we're nowhere near Halloween.

A big part of training is figuring out what you like so you leave nothing to chance on race day. Right now, I plan to eat a CLIF Bar on my way to the trail head. I'll have Hammer Gel, GU Chomps, GU Packets, CLIF SHOTS and CLIF BLOKS (energy chews) close by.

I will consume additional calories at miles six, 11 and 15.

And I'm praying to God that nothing tears up my stomach, makes me queasy or gives me the sh*ts.

I woke up today so not feeling a run. It was snowing, so Midas and I geared up and headed out. I wore the CAT hat, a visor (to keep the snow off my face), my headlamp and a hood. Yep, so thankful I'm not looking for a husband.

Best Way Out? Through.

Most days, I fly out of bed ready to kick the world's a**.

But this week, I've been sluggish. My shins hurt. And the top of my left foot is on fire. This doesn't mean I'm a quitter. It just means there will be times when this proves to be a hell of a struggle.

I got this message from a fellow sole sister on Facebook yesterday:

"Your first marathon is your worst and your best. You worry all the way round, swear you will never do it again, but are hooked from the minute you get the medal! I'm a late starter, but said I would only ever do one, I've done 10 and I am doing five this year. You'll be great, have faith."

A small part of me wanted to spiral when I read this.

I thought, "Oh f*. Five marathons? In a year? It's taking everything I have to do one."

(See what happens when we compare ourselves to others? So if you're comparing yourself to me, please stop.)

But another part of me was so damn thankful this lady's in my corner telling me I'll be great and to have faith.

The "social" piece of this journey has been just as important as logging the miles.

- Midas gets me up and out the door every day.

- The blog keeps me telling the story..

- The love on Facebook inspires me to do sh*t that sometimes, I just don't want to do.

I talk a lot (in my business) about leadership.

But the message that's been haunting me this week is, "You have to show people. Do the work. Tell the truth. Stay loyal to what you said you'd do long after the mood you said it in has left you."

And folks, there are some days my "Be a Marathoner" mood has completely *vacated* this house.

This adventure has been a wild, unpredictable, soulful, crazy-a** ride.

Not every day has been (or will be!) perfect.

But Robert Frost said it best: "The best way out is always through."

So through I'll go.

Midas and I put up four miles this morning. It was so all about him. Stop. Go. Stop. Go. Pee. Go. Stop. Pee. Go. Ugh.

"You're Just Big Boned"

Day 55

I was an overweight kid.

I remember in 4th grade thinking Velveeta was its own food group. I loved chicken-fried steak, tater-tots, ice cream, basically anything with loads of fat and sugar.

I'd bike home from school, grab a bag of generic cheese snacks, a sugary fruit drink and head to the basement for my daily dose of She-Ra and Scooby-Doo.

When I complained about my weight, my Dad would say, "Oh Brook, you're just big-boned."

(Thanks, Dad.)

At my heaviest I tipped the scales at 160.

For some people this will sound like a champagne problem, I know. But for MY frame, it was too much extra weight to carry.

I share this because today, thanks to marathon training, I'm probably in the best shape of my life.

- I can finally see my abs. (Okay, I can see my *ribs*. My abs are nowhere to be found. But a girl can dream.)

- You can bounce a quarter off my quads. (And my calves, but only because they are so freakin' tight from overuse.)

The only thing that hasn't changed is the size of my a**.

This is the absolute truth. It's the same damn size it was before I started training.

No one believes me when say I used to be heavy because all they see now is a girl rockin' her skinny jeans, chasing a big marathon dream.

I've met dozens of people who want to train for a marathon to lose weight. I've also met people who throw a marathon out as their New Year's resolution. (Does either of these reasons actually work?)

Me? I had to dig deeper.

I had to go all the way to rock bottom on a number of things in my life, first.

Once I got there, I took a good look around and asked, "Okay self. How in the f* are we going to get out of here?"

Run a marathon.

Now you know.

I'm sharing this story today because dozens of you have emailed me asking for motivation or tips on how to get started. To steal a quote from the Biggest Loser: It takes a while for your body to change, but it only takes a split-second to change your mind. Make today the day you change your mind.

Big Girl Pants? Check.

I've been freakin' emotional this week.

Yesterday, I knew it was time for this chica to pull her sh*t together.

So, I did what all girls do when it's time to get over our drama and back in the saddle: I headed out for a massage and an eyebrow wax.

I've heard having your brows waxed helps you run faster and takes 10 years off your face. A total win-win.

After I stumbled out of the massage room, the therapist directed me to the lobby and told me to sit and wait for the queen of all things wax to fetch me.

Um, yeah. Here's what happens next: The f*ing fire alarm starts to blast.

I'm like, "Hey. Hey? HEY! HEY! HEY! Is there a fire?"

Part of me wanted to hit the deck and roll around, you know, kind of get in the spirit of things. The other part wanted to pull the f*ing ugly bang clip from my hair and stand tall in case a Denver fireman wanted to *rescue* me. No sale.

I did not roll around and I wasn't even *close* to being rescued. It was a fire-drill. Such a bummer.

Still craving a bit more self-love therapy, I went out for dinner.

1) I didn't have to cook and

2) I completely rocked the carbs.

3) I also splurged on an after dinner treat: caramel sea salt gelato. Just ask me if I feel bad.

My attitude has turned the corner. My big girl pants are back on with a vengeance. And I'm ready to rock the road for 18 big ones tomorrow.

Training for a marathon is like having a baby (with a bit shorter gestation period). I cry, laugh, get pissed, roll around on the floor, pout ... you catch my drift. Thanks for hangin' with me this week.

No Turning Back

My first full year of running, I felt like a fraud.

For a long time, I was embarrassed about how slow I ran. My terrible form. The ratty gear I threw on every day at the a** crack of dawn. The fact that I didn't brush my chicklets before leaving the house.

(Note: I DO brush my teeth on long run days, I don't think I could bear it for that long.)

Sans Midas, I have done every single long run (in my life!) alone. So today was a first. I ran with my good friend Andi, who's training for the same marathon. It will be her fourth time laying down 26.2. (Sweet Mother of Pearl.)

Before I dive into the deets (and lessons), I thought you should know that I ran right up to 18 miles and kicked it squarely in the a**. I think I even had a few miles in me to spare. I ran across the final bridge and hollered out, "Woo hoo! I am so f*ing proud of myself! ROAR! ROAR! ROAR! (Ridiculous, I know.)

All that said, here are today's lessons:

- Running with someone who is stronger, (Andi, in my case), leaves you no other choice but to bring your A-game. We ran 18 miles in three hours and 10 minutes, a new personal best for me.

- I'd rather be cold than hot. My first few miles were sluggish because I was too warm and could not focus.

- Next week, I will use two pieces of duct-tape to secure my ear buds. Today's tape worked its way down to my right boob. Not cool.

- Against my better judgment, I wore an Under Armour shirt. I didn't end up with a midriff, but for the love of all things holy, can someone please tell me WTF I'm doing wrong?

- FOR GIRLS ONLY: Bleeding sucks. While having your period is no excuse, I'm telling you, it affects your energy level (and your need to find a bathroom).

- There was a heated public restroom open at mile 9.5. Someone up top had my back.

- The magic happens during new miles. Between miles 16 and 18 (my new miles), I paid close attention to my body. Where it hurt, what it needed and what I might do differently next time.

Something happened out there today. I no longer feel like a fraud. I am ridiculously proud of myself.

And there's no turning back.

From today on, I will always be a girl who ran a mean 18 miles without puking, fainting or dying.

I'm not quite ready to run a marathon.

But I will be.

I cried six times on my run, and I have tears in my eyes right now. Thank you for witnessing my transformation and for being strong enough to ignite your own. I'm honored you're along on this ride.

A Prison Break

Midas got me up at 4:30 this morning.

Good freakin' night! I guess no one told him I ran 18 miles yesterday. Not that he cares; he was pretty peeved when I pulled out of the driveway without him.

I laid in bed for a full 10 minutes before my feet hit the deck.

1. I needed to make sure my legs were still attached.

2. When I realized they were, (surprise, surprise), I had to move them around a bit to get the blood flowing again.

The lesson I forgot to mention yesterday is that no matter how good I feel after a long run, the next day I always have a John Wayne swagger.

The only way I know to get over feeling terrible is to get movin'.

So that's what Midas and I did.

I threw on my freshly-washed-all-things-Downy-smellin'-gear, strapped on our lamps, (yes, Midas has a Puplight!), attached the leash and out the door we went.

Note: The person who invented the Puplight is likely sitting his/her a** on a beach in a faraway land, while we bang it out in 20 degree weather. F*ing genius.

I share the Puplight because today, Midas's light was set on disco, but there is no disco setting. Our first half-mile felt like a prison break. (Think strobe light flashing right in your bloody eyes.) Umm, yeah. Not today. I wasn't in the mood to play John Travolta or a fugitive so I turned his Puplight off.

The batteries in my headlamp are almost dead, so we were left pretty much in the dark. And let me tell you, running at 4:30 a.m. with no light is like running across the moon's surface blindfolded.

I tripped on every speed bump in my neighborhood. (There are 14.)

My left foot landed in the same hole on the way out and on the way back.

Somewhere close the midway point I thought I had run into barbwire. (On the street.) I kept thinking, "WTF?" I tried to run through it for a few steps but a poke in the shin stopped me. A closer look revealed I was wrestling with a tree branch.

We set out to run four miles this morning. But in truth, we walked at least a mile. Every time Midas wanted to stop, pee or sniff, I was all too happy to let him. (It took us 56 minutes to finish four miles. No world record here.)

While I'm all about gettin' a move on, I'm also about letting Midas be a dog.

Oh yes, and I'm all for my weary legs catching a much-needed break.

A peek in the bathroom mirror revealed my shirt was on backwards this morning. Did I mention I am damn thankful no one else was around?

R-E-S-P-E-C-T

Yesterday, I knew I had work to do.

D.R. and I only have rendezvous points identified through mile seven (and back) on my trail. If I'm going to run 20 and 22 in the very near future — it was time to scout new locations.

So Hubs and I headed out for a death march on our bikes. (As if running 18 miles on Saturday wasn't enough, we put up 17 miles on our bikes yesterday. Good freakin' night.)

It was sunny and fabulous, so we worked our way down the trail.

Let me tell you, I'm no speed racer.

I'm cruising along, minding my own business, when a big burly guy who was far too big for his bike, passes me and yells out, "I like your 29s!"

As I was eating his dust, I thought to myself, "WTH? My a** is way bigger than 29 inches." It took me a full minute to realize he was talking about my bike tires. Smart man.

Further down, there was another guy pounding it out in the dirt. I'm telling you, his mouth was open so freakin' wide I could see his molars. He was half smiling and half gasping for air. It reminded me of how Midas looks when he hangs his head out the car window and his mouth catches wind. Hilarious!

When we reached our final destination, (10.5 miles from where I start my runs), I stopped to take a good look around and thought, "Okay self. This is what's waiting for us on our last long run before the race."

I was kind of hoping the trail would lead right up to Ryan Gosling' back door, or that there'd be a carnival in my honor. Heck, I'd settle for a well-lit public restroom and a vending machine.

It's a wide-open field.

There is comfort in knowing where I'm headed and what to expect. You know, like where I'll see D.R. in case I blow it, bag it or just need a bathroom.

Am I highly structured? Hell yes.

Borderline anal? Probably.

We turned around and pedaled back to the car. A few miles from the finish, I came up behind a 70-something-year-old guy on his bicycle that looked like it, (the bike, not him), had seen better days. While passing, I noticed the transistor radio strapped to his handle bars.

As I cruised by I heard Aretha Franklin belting out R-E-S-P-E-C-T.

And in that moment, I felt a great deal of respect for the road, this journey and myself.

People often ask, "Hey Brook, what are you doing this weekend?" Um, yeah. Nothing. Honestly, from here until race day almost every weekend revolves around running and recovery. I know it's totally lame, but it's true.

Brook:1. Bug: 0.

This morning, as I stood inside my closet, I could hear the wind howling.

Midas and I were up at 4:50 a.m. As I stumbled in to get dressed, I thought, Oh f*. We're going to take a beating.

(Hint: We did.)

Rarely one to call a run because of weather, I layered up and we headed out.

It totally irritates me when the wind blows in my face every time I run uphill. But today, it blew in my face downhill, too. Everywhere I turned it was still in my face.

With the wind's help, today I ate my first bug of the season.

ACK.

I contemplated who won that battle, me or the bug. Was it me because he got gnashed by my chicklets and ended up in my stomach, or was it him because he hit me head on in the first place?

Bugs = Spring. So I suppose it's all good.

*Someone sent me this quote and I want to share it with you: "You don't get it by staring. You don't get it by wishing. You don't get it by hoping. You don't get it easy. You get it by getting off your a** and working for it every second of every day for the rest of your life."*

3 Miles Per Hour

A year ago, I met the first woman to walk around the world.

To say Polly Letofsky's story is inspiring is the understatement of the century. If you think training for a marathon is heroic, just wait until you read this.

Her five-year adventure took her 14,124 miles across 22 countries in North America, Australia, Asia and Europe. She walked an average of three miles per hour, 15 miles each day. For 1,825 consecutive days.

As if she wasn't busy enough, she also raised more than $250,000 for 13 breast cancer organizations. Oh yeah, and burned through 29 pairs of shoes.

Polly's journey was on my mind this morning. While wrestling with my compression socks, (which take seven full minutes to remove — plenty of time to solve the world's problems), I thought about how long it takes to train for a marathon.

My training schedule is five months.

Some days it feels like I just started, and others days it feels like I'll be training forever. But five months is nowhere near five years -- thank God Almighty. If it took five years to train for a marathon, I know I'd bail.

Yesterday, someone asked me, "Do you have any advice for a newbie? I just started running three years ago and my long race last year was a half marathon."

My response? "Brother, asking me for advice is like the blind leading the blind. It's my first, too! The best I can say is don't skimp on your training miles, eat really, really well and love the journey."

Today, I'm celebrating the fact that small steps every day net big results. And I'd like to give a special shout out to Polly for proving that it's true.

Yesterday was the half-way point — I celebrated by buying myself a new pair of cowgirl boots. When a girl has more running shoes than sassy shoes, she simply has to fix it.

Avoiding the Hotel Dreadmill

Day 62

Right now, I'm on a plane zooming toward the Midwest.

I'm heading home for my parent's 30th Anniversary party. Can you freakin' imagine spending 30 years with the same person? Sometimes 30 days feels heroic.

I always run when I travel. But this feels like new territory. I've never changed time zones while "training for a marathon."

My online inquisition last night produced some helpful tips for how to run while you're on the road. (Note: Some I loved. Some I bagged. But they're all definitely worth a quick read-through.)

BK's TOP 9 Tips For Running On The Run

1) Run in the Morning. If you get it over with early, it won't interfere with your activities. (I love this – and you already know I'm a morning runner. I will proceed with cocktail hour(s) as scheduled.)

2) Scale Back. Experts say one of the biggest hurdles to running while traveling is over committing. You only need to run enough to keep up the habit and reinforce your condition. (While I understand this theory, I'm bagging it. My plan is to up my mileage because Midas isn't making the trip.)

3) Take Extra Gear. You never know when you'll have access to laundry facilities. (I am taking all of my outdoor running gear. Unfortunately, not one article I read mentioned "plan on paying the damn airlines check bag fee.")

4) Don't Party Too Hard. One author penned, "This doesn't mean no drinking, but you might consider filling every other glass with water." (It's been a long time since I've had a cocktail at sea-level. Can't you drink more and suffer less?!?!)

5) Plan Your Route. Try using Gmaps Pedometer or MapMyRun. Make sure your route is simple enough that you can actually remember how to get back. (I'm no stranger to being lost on a run.) For longer runs, consider a route that takes you back to home base at least once.

(I'm covered here. I think I'll be able to lap the entire town on Saturday's outing.)

6) Stay Alert. Leave your iPod at home and take in the surroundings. (Umm, no. Ditching this travel tip, too. I can't run more than two miles without music.)

7) Have Resources. Consider carrying a phone and a credit card. (This one seemed like a no-brainer. I always keep plastic or cash close so I can "buy" my way out of trouble if need be.)

8) Eat and Drink Right. You never know when your next meal will be, and traveling dehydrates you.

9) Take snacks and snag a water at the airport. (Listen. I go two miles from home and stash six snacks in my purse. Brook hungry = white hot mess. Same goes for water. Half my suitcase is CLIF bars. Praying the baggage handlers don't sniff them out.)

I can hardly stand to run on a hotel dreadmill. (Treadmill.)

So I had no choice. I checked my bag and trusted my coveted running gear to total strangers.

If it all goes to plan, you won't hear any more about this. If not, Frontier Airlines won't know what hit them.

Hubs is out of town. He called last night and said, "Hey, did you get a new pair of boots?" My reply was, um...yes? Listen ladies, you know there are things you don't tell your husband. My new boots were one of them. BUSTED.

Organizing Hookers

I am a simple girl from Nebraska.

I drive a Toyota 4-Runner that's nearly eight-years old. It was the first vehicle I owned that had a CD player and 4-wheel drive. It has 120k hard-earned miles on its V6 engine. Trust me, it's seen better days.

I rolled up to Budget Rental yesterday (at my destination) and the clerk says, "Sorry, we don't have any vehicles left in the you're-a-cheap-a** category."

I said, "What do you have?"

She says, "A Dodge Charger, 8-cylinder with a bangin' stereo, sub-woofers in the trunk, tricked out wheels, GPS, satellite stereo and a HEMI engine."

The Nebraska girl in me croaks back, "Is that rear-wheel drive?" (Like I even know what the f* that means.) It's supposed to snow a few inches and I have "heard" rear-wheel drive sucks in snow.

"It is rear wheel drive," she says as she rolls her eyes.

And in that moment, the dare-devil, NASCAR-loving Dannika Patrick in me said, "I'll take it."

Off I go. Fittingly, Macklemore's song Thrift Shop was blaring on the radio. I think to myself, "I would be so freakin' good at being wealthy."

Within minutes, my buns start to heat up and I wonder to myself just what the hell is going on. It crosses my mind that either 1) I peed my pants or that 2) I pulled a butt cheek muscle while throwing my Texas-sized suitcase in the trunk. It takes me three full minutes to realize the car has seat-warmers.

I told you what I drive so you can see the disconnect.

A little further down the road I felt the same warming sensation under my hands. The car has hand-warmers. In the freakin' steering wheel. And in that moment, I wept. I realized all I'm missing by not having a car like this waiting for me after my sub-freezing long runs.

Hey, you don't know what you don't know. The problem is now I do.

I roll up to my brother's house and he comes out to grab my suitcase. I roll down the window and holler out, "I look like a hooker!" He says, "No, Brook, you look like someone who *organizes* hookers."

Hmmm.

I met up with an old friend last night to catch up on everything that's new and good. She invited her niece along, a 21-year-old college student who has the world by the balls. A few minutes into the conversation, I asked if she was a runner. (I am developing a 6th sense for sole sisters.)

Turns out she just ran her first ever 5k last weekend. Awesome, right?

A small part of me was envious. Not of her, or the 5k, but the fact that she just turned 21. I secretly wondered what it would be like to be training for a marathon at 21 instead of 36. I think it might hurt a hell-of-a-lot less.

In that moment, I knew I would never have trained for a marathon at 21. Because the truth is, who I am now is so much different than who I was then.

It took a series of perfectly orchestrated events for me to be here doing this.

And for me, now is right on time.

This morning I tried scotch tape to keep my ear buds in place. Don't bother. I'm off to rock the road in my HEMI 'cause that's how girls from Nebraska roll.

One in Every City

Some women have men in every city.

I happen to have Chiropractors.

My aching bones beg to be cracked, twisted and yanked on at least once a week. If I don't do chiropractic, I pay dearly on my next long run. It's my body's not-so-funny way of keeping me honest and on my A-game.

Wherever I am in the world, if it's Friday, you can bet your a** I'm on the hunt for the very best doctor I can find.

Lucky me, I found one.

During my adjustment yesterday, the good doctor said, "Hey, I can tell you're under consistent care – your back looks great and it wants to be in alignment." Music to my freakin' ears.

(Note: My adjustment came *after* they told me I had to fill out a patient chart. Part of establishing a chart is to have your blood pressure taken. They also weigh you.)

The truth is, I can't stand to step on the scale. But begrudgingly, I got on. And I said to the assistant, "Okay, lady. If it's over this number, please don't tell me." So I stepped on the scale and her mouth stayed shut.

SH*T! SH*T! SH*T!

"By how much?" I implored. "Two pounds," she whispered.

The kid in me wanted to throw off all of my clothes and have a "do over." I also wanted to reason with her (or the scale, whatever). I just ate lunch! I'm more bloated in the afternoon! I've been traveling! There are 612 reasons I'm over my goal weight and none of them are my fault!

You'll be impressed to know I did none of those things. I kept my mouth closed.

Which leads me to today.

I squeezed in a 10-mile run — my longest ever on the road.

Here's what I learned:

- You will never put up a personal best when there is ice and/or snow on the sidewalk.

- Front desk people will think you're crazy when you ask them for a piece of scotch tape and then proceed to apply it, (to your chest area, over your ear bud wires), before you walk out the door.

- It's nice to know people in the area. I made a pit stop at mile four and picked up a Nutri-grain bar for free.

- No matter how many CLIF Bars you cram into your suitcase, you still eat like sh*t when you don't have access to your own kitchen.

- It's super easy to meet new people on the run. I walked right up to a small group of sole sisters and asked if I could take their picture. They too thought I was crazy. I'm sure I'll make the local newspaper tomorrow: "Freak on the loose in a Cat hat."

It's been more difficult to run while traveling than I thought. I'm busy seeing peeps, I'm not sleeping as well, and the change in time zones has definitely made a difference.

I'm still on track to run six, 10, six, but it feels heroic.

I have one last hurrah tonight: My primary reason for this trip.

I've loved every single moment of my time here. But as Dorothy says, "There's no place like home."

I discovered another weakness last night: fancy mixed nuts. I have a two-pound bag sitting in my hotel room. But seriously, I've probably already eaten half of them. I may get in trouble but I don't care. They called to me, and I needed them.

Two False Starts

Last night was the actual party to celebrate my parent's 30th Anniversary.

I'm not going to lie – I probably drank one too many cocktails. So when my alarm went off at 5:15 a.m., I rolled around for 20 minutes cursing the gods who make the nighttime hours zip by.

When I did finally crawl my a** out of bed, I put on all of my outdoor running gear, and headed for the car.

Folks, let me tell you, the Midwest is a different kind of cold. When the wind blows, it freakin' howls. And 22 degrees feels like minus 100 because of the humidity.

I sat in the car, turned it on and thought, "What the f* are you doing? There's a treadmill inside. Get your tail back in there and use it."

So, I got out of the car and started walking toward the front door of the hotel.

On the short trip back inside, I started to feel guilty. I thought to myself, "You never call a run for weather! You can do this! It's been cold before, turn your a** around and get in that car."

So I did. I even started the car a second time for good measure.

But again, a small voice said, "You don't have to run outside. The hotel has a treadmill. You did bring some lightweight running gear.

A war went on in my mind for several minutes.

I got back out of the car, walked up to my room, changed into my indoor running gear and went directly to the fitness center. I pounded out six miles on that bloody treadmill.

The interesting part was I could see my neck in the TV monitor attached to the machine. For an hour I "watched" myself sweat. It crossed my mind that I am sweating out the old me.

That felt awesome.

I've realized today that it takes a team of people for me to train for a marathon. The chiropractor here kept my legs connected to my brain. My mom washed my running clothes (twice!) and answered her door when I stopped by on yesterday's run to grab a snack. My brother gave me lots of laughs with his comment, "You look like someone who organizes hookers."

Today, I'm offering up thanks that there are a whole lot of peeps willing to go out of their way to make sure I reach my goal.

I'm humbled. And I hope to one day repay the favor.

I'll be zipping back to Omaha shortly to catch my flight back to Denver. Watch for me in the smokin' hot Dodge Charger. A part of me feels like I'll be leaving a piece of my identity at Budget Rental today.

I'm an exceedingly modest person.

I always color within the lines. I'm 1,000 percent a God-fearing girl. I never stray too far from the law. (Unless I'm in a Dodge Charger, then it's game on.)

So back in January, when I asked Hubs to take my pre-marathon training photos neked, he thought maybe I had turned a new leaf. Not quite. But, I am all about setting benchmarks.

I want to know if:

- 500 miles over five months will tighten my buns.

- Help me lose those pesky extra pounds.

- If all this training will actually change my physical appearance. (It better.)

So I stood in my walk-in closet, shut my eyes and said, "Hurry up."

Let me tell you, my closet is the only room in my house that has florescent lights. And there ain't a person on the planet who looks good neked under florescent lights. I took photos of Hubs neked, too. (He was going to train for the marathon, but he's opted for the half.)

After our ridiculously weird photo shoot, I took a quick peek at the pictures. OH f*. They're terrible. There's really no other way to say it.

I've rarely thought about those photos. I didn't plan on revisiting them again until after the marathon to compare the before and after.

All that changed last Saturday night at my Parents' 30th Anniversary party.

When dozens of family members you haven't seen in years get together, what happens?

The cameras come out in full force. Here's how it went down: I handed over my phone to my brother, Tom. I ask him to take a picture of me with my brother Beau. He starts pushing all kinds of buttons.

Within seconds, he looks at me with total fear and mortification in his eyes. He says, "Oh f* Brook. I just saw a neked man's a** on your camera."

He launches the phone at me and says, "Hey lady, I didn't bargain for this. I don't know what I just saw — but it left me f*ing blind." I look down at my phone and realize he's just seen a pic of hub's bare a**.

I couldn't explain fast enough.

No, we are not into pornography. No, the altitude hasn't adversely affected us. No, we don't roll that way. No, we're not a bunch of crazies who live in Denver so our families don't know just how off our rockers we truly are.

Needless to say, I never did get that picture with my brother Beau. But we did get something we will laugh our a**es off about for many years to come.

So, back to benchmarks: I'm measuring a lot of different things. I've been tracking miles, my weight, inches lost and overall physical changes. But I wish I had done more.

If I could go back, I would have done a bone density test. (Before and after.) I would have had blood drawn. (Also before and after.) I also would have measured every body part I could get a measuring tape around. (Calves, quads, arms, forearms, waist, boobs, rib cage, hips — everything.)

For me, monitoring the physical changes is super important. But even more important is what's happening on the inside. I've reconnected with my swagger. My confidence is at an all-time high. I feel strong. Powerful. Capable. Almost invincible.

I tell everyone if you want to change your life, train for a marathon. The cool part is, it's the truth.

*Midas and I headed out in -1 degree temps this morning. God bless that's cold. It was a rest day so we took a leisurely walk around the neighborhood. Albeit, when it's that f*ing cold there ain't nothing leisurely about it.*

FREE RESOURCE: It's super important to track your measurements so you can see how much you change physically while training. Download your free Measurement Mastery Worksheet at www.MarathonTrainingTools.com.

The Truth About Days Off

Yesterday should have been a REST day.

The busy bee in me has a hell of a time complying with rest days. Rest? Who needs rest? I need to shake my a** to make race day in tip top shape, right?

Maybe not.

While working on my marathon training schedule a few months ago, I was chatting up my good friend who is all things marathon. Think semi-pro athlete, trains other athletes, knows everything there is to know about how your body works, what it needs, etc.

She encouraged me to decrease my miles every few weeks to give my body time to recover. Part of her wisdom felt like a blessing. After all, who wants to put up 18 freakin' miles every Saturday for months on end?

But a small part of me was upset.

I am a Type-A personality. I can't stand to go backwards. Hell, I can't even stand to stay even. I want to push and push and push and push until my body either cries out or breaks. (As I share this I'm wondering if I also have a screw loose. It could explain a lot.)

The truth is, I won't even make it to the starting line on race day if I'm sick, broken-down, burned-out or half dead.

I hit up a few websites last night to see if I could figure out why I detest rest days. Turns out, I'm not alone. Nearly everything I read proved most athletes struggle with taking days off.

Here's why I struggle with days off:

- I feel LAZY.

- A small part of me doesn't believe I've earned it.

- Some of my self-worth is tied to my level of productivity each day.

- It's in my DNA to go until I crash and then find a way back.

- I don't feel I can eat what I want if I don't run at least three miles per day.

All of my reasons are total bull sh*t. And they're mostly mental, not physical.

But I'm finally catching on, albeit slowly, that there's a difference between being a runner and being a mature runner.

Begrudgingly, I'm crossing that bridge.

Three months ago I swore I'd do whatever it takes to lay down 26.2 without walking, crawling, puking, or dying.

And if that means taking a few days off, so be it.

Yesterday, I had to force Hubs to read what I wrote about his bare a**. I'm laughing out loud while he's scrolling down the page. He looks at me and says, "This would be a lot funnier if it was about someone else's a**." Touché.

I own seven sports bras.

Four Nike, two Champion and one Lululemon. (Two of the Nike bras are older than Jesus, so they hit the trash today immediately after being counted.)

My fluorescent pink Nike bra is a souvenir from Mexico. I forgot to take a sports bra with me on vacation — I actually gave my bikini top a try on the treadmill. Um, no. The Champions I picked up before my first half marathon last year. They are the same damn size, but one is way too tight. And the Lululemon was an impulse buy after my first full-on war with chafing.

A few weeks ago, I shared that I was on a mission to save the girls. (My Ziploc plan turned armband.) That's where we established I literally have no boobs.

I'm a 34B. Honestly, I'm probably a 34A, but I am a 36-year-old grown woman. I refuse to claim A status.

Right now, I am thankful beyond measure that my boobs are small. I've read zillions of books and articles written by women who are rockin' a D and keeping their girls close by layering two bras.

I've had three major challenges with sports bras:

1. The elastic band around my rib cage stretches out and offers zero support.

2. The elastic band around my rib cage is too freakin' tight.

3. When a sports bra is too tight, it causes chafing. Not to mention the fact that I can't breathe.

My favorite bra is made by Champion. That said, I think it all comes down to your girls.

Note: I don't believe money or brand name has anything to do with what works.

Some people spend hundreds on bras; others pick their bras up at Wal-Mart. The most I have spent to-date on one of these crazy contraptions is $56.

I have, however, discovered the super secretive, easy to apply, quick-fix formula for chafing.

Deodorant.

Before every long run, I bust out the Secret Powder Fresh and put that sh*t everywhere. And by everywhere, I mean everywhere. Shoulders, underarms, rib cage, back, every place a sliver of spandex touches my body. (It works.)

It's game on when it comes to my girls. Because I'm all about savin' what the good Lord gave me.

I put up four miles with Midas this morning. I have ordered him a new Puplight; we just missed a head on collision with another runner/dog duo.

Howling Cuss Words

You have to respect the road, or the road won't respect you.

Eighteen months ago, while visiting my parents, I set out for an early morning run. I was mid-stride, about a mile from their house, when my left foot landed squarely on top of a boulder. (OK, it was a small piece of gravel. But, let me tell the story.)

SNAP! Oh f*.

I hopped around in circles on my right foot for a full minute, howling every cuss word I knew. I even made up a few new words for good measure 'cause that's how I roll. I hobbled along for a few steps and figured out I was in deep sh*t.

In that moment, I had a choice to make: I could call it quits and limp back to their house or I could keep running. Here's what went through my mind: "Sister, you'd better keep truckin'. This is the last run you're going to have for a very long time."

So the dip sh*t in me kept going. I put up just over five miles that day. And I didn't run again for six full weeks. I'd like to tell you I'm so much smarter now, but honestly, I'd probably make the same choice again.

Turns out I broke a metatarsal bone. The podiatrist said it's a fairly common injury for runners.

I didn't know this, but the human body contains 206 bones, 26 in each foot and ankle, which means both feet combined make up 25 percent of the total number of bones in your body. No wonder runners break bones in their feet. I suppose it's better than breaking your a**.

Never one to stop moving, I walked Midas three miles every day in my boot, no less, for the entire six weeks.

I share this because every single time my left foot hits a pothole -- which is freakin' daily in my neighborhood -- I think about what could happen.

Does it concern me? Hell, yes.

Does it stop me? Hell, no.

Training for my first marathon has given me a whole new appreciation for the road.

I'm awed that it's always free, available, open and ready. It greets me like an old friend. It never complains and it consistently provides a level of comfort I've yet to find anywhere else.

I have learned that if I show respect for the road, it respects me right back.

I pushed Midas a little farther this morning on our run (4.8 miles). When we turned around to run the same leg twice he stopped, looked at me and said, "WTF Mom?" He made it, but I think I maxed him out.

Pre-Game Checklist

I bang out my long runs on Saturdays.

This means for the last thirteen weeks, Friday's have been all about the pre-game strategy. When I have a long run looming, I obsess about it all week. I visualize miles two, five and 7. I think about what it will feel like to turn around at the official halfway point. Finally, I get into the magic of running down the home stretch.

But obsessing about the miles is only part of the equation. There are a zillion other things I do to prepare:

- Email D.R. every Thursday to determine our plan of attack. This involves a few e-mails back and forth and detailed information on rendezvous locations.

- Pre-plan the Friday night meal, which from here until race day will be a grilled chicken breast, baked potato and salad. I tried pasta; the sodium in the sauce almost killed me.

- Select my outfit based on weather and mileage. (Diva? I'll own that.)

- Confirm my chiropractic appointment.

Here's how Friday's go down:

- Wake up and head out for a walk or a short run with Midas. (No more than three miles.)

- While getting ready, I make sure my toenails are cut. (This totally matters — don't skip this step.)

- I shave my legs, at least from the knees down. My chiro doesn't get paid enough to deal with all that.

- I throw my running gear in the wash. Might as well start out smelling Downy fresh; it certainly doesn't end that way.

- I head over to the chiropractor's office and actually pay him to abuse me. He digs in to my calves until I cry, yet, I continue to go. Something about that just isn't right.

The rest of the day is work, work, work.

After dinner, I spend 20-plus minutes laying out snacks and gear. This includes mace, my arm band, CAT hat, neck warmer, water, gloves ... in other words, every last thing I think I might need over the course of the run. I also make sure my phone is fully charged so I can use MapMyRun to track miles, time, incline, etc.

Training runs are designed to do one thing: Prepare you for race day.

And every week, I feel closer to ready.

I'm up for 18 tomorrow – hooboy. Let's roll.

FREE RESOURCE: Get the fool-proof checklist for remembering everything you need for your long runs. Download your free Pre-Game Checklist at www.MarathonTrainingTools.com.

Know When To Fold 'Em

Today I bagged my 18-mile run at mile 14.

I know. F*. I'm not a gambler, but it appears that this morning, I was clean out of aces.

What I'm about to share is gross. But in the spirit of transparency, I'm going to give it to you straight.

Last night, I was up at 3 a.m. with a mild case of heartburn. Always the optimist, I thought, cool. I'll take a little white pill, drink some water and be ready to roll. A few hours later, I got up and got dressed.

I started to feel all secret agent and sh*t.

I used two pieces of Hello Kitty duct tape to keep my ear buds in place -- one above the bra, one below.

I laughed to myself and thought of Ginger in Swordfish – I'm DEA Stanley!

Listen. If Hugh Jackman is in the room and I'm half neked, I'd probably dive for the bathroom door. Or for him. It's anybody's guess. But, I digress.

Driving to the trail, a white unmarked van rolls up next to me at the stoplight. And I thought, bring it mister. I've got some bad a** moves I've been *dying* to try. He didn't even look over; I obviously was in no danger.

I finally made it to the starting line, gave D.R. a quick hug, handed her the goods and off I went.

I blew by mile two – no problem. Between miles three and five, I began to burp. Think little burps – just a nuisance. Between miles seven and nine, I started to puke a little with every burp. Around mile 10, I hit the restroom, ditched some gear and looked D.R. straight in the eye.

"I'm f*ed," I said. "I have heartburn like a mother f*er." Never one to call a run unless death is imminent, I kept going. Mile 12 is where it all blew up.

I'm running at a snail's pace. I know I need to puke. I know I'll feel a zillion times better if I do. So my legs and I pull over to try and work sh*t out. My mouth was dripping saliva. So I spit. And I kept spitting. I stood there for 90 seconds knowing a good purge was milliseconds away.

I squatted down. (I didn't want to splash myself.)

I plugged my nose. (I can't stand the feeling of puke blasting through my nostrils.)

And finally, nothing. Just a lot more saliva.

I was trailside for three or four minutes. Thankfully, no one ran by. Albeit my give-a-damn at that point was broken. I just wanted to feel better. I pulled myself up, got back on the trail and jogged/walked/crawled back to D.R. I knew I was finished.

I've bagged two long runs training for this marathon. The first was five weeks ago on a 14-er. The second was today. Part of me is so crazy pissed that I'm nearly sick. The other part is super thankful there are still seven weeks left to train. That also gives me plenty of time to figure out what's giving me all this stinkin' heartburn.

So, I am moving my training schedule around a bit. I'll try 18 miles again next Saturday. In the meantime, I am taking Kenny Roger's advice:

You've got to know when to hold 'em. Know when to fold 'em. Know when to walk away. Know when to run.

Opting For Quality

If I could run 7 days a week with zero consequence I would.

But people who are much smarter than me say cross training (CT) strengthens your non-running muscles. It also helps you avoid injury. Do you think it helps with heartburn? Freakin' doubtful.

Never one to buck authority, my marathon training schedule includes one day per week of CT. I wish I could tell you I go all Om on Sundays, but I don't. I tried yoga. I tried Pilates. Zumba is probably more my speed, but I worry I'd break my a** pretending to be JLo.

My CT is usually a bike ride or a hike. Yesterday was a hike; Hubs and Midas came along, too. It felt like a strong way to close out March before tallying up my miles.

Last month, I shared that March worried me most. That's why I'm beyond thankful I made it to April without my legs falling off. Here's how the numbers shook out:

March	Total-To-Date
Ran: 157.60 miles	Running: 396.19 miles
Walked: 26.7 miles	Walking: 82.71 miles
Hiked: 4 miles	Hiking: 12 miles
Biked: 24	Biking: 48.5
Midas Total: 94.5 R/W/H	Midas T-T-D: 246.74

March was not without incident: Think extraterrestrials. My first 16-mile run, then my first 18. A custom-made pee machine. Switching time zones. Too many meltdowns to count. My first bug of the season. Neked pictures. Sports bras. Broken bones. Puking. Heartburn.

When I look at these numbers, I'm surprised this sh*t hasn't killed me.

But in truth, every single hard-earned step has made me *stronger.*

I could take every training shortcut there is. You know, like half a** my miles. Eat like sh*t. Be extra hard on my body.

But the only person I'd be screwing is myself.

So I'm opting for quality. And I'll continue to rack up the miles.

Because that's just how I roll.

Running Into Crazy

I'm an annoyingly happy person.

I wake up every single day with sunshine shooting out of my eyeballs.

When I was young, my mom would wake me up singing "Zip-A-Dee-Doo-Dah." At the same time, she'd dig my midget legs out from under the covers and crack my toes. I have no doubt this simple morning ritual changed my DNA. I know it changed the shape of my freakin' toes.

This morning when Midas and I headed out for four miles, it was foggy and damp.

It put me in a somber, reflective mood.

Never one to run without my Shuffle, I traveled around the world and down memory lane in just 43 minutes. Courtesy of Apple and my playlist.

This is why I'm starting to think I might be crazy.

The first song to bellow in my ears was Bop by Dan Seals. This song reminds me of two things. The first is the Armory in my hometown, where everyone who was anyone held their wedding reception. (I'm from a small town, no judging.) It also reminds me of 1986, the year the Space Shuttle Challenger blew up. Deep and weird, I know.

Next up? Lady Gaga's You and I. Her lyrics, "There's only three men that I must serve my whole life; it's the Dalai and Nebraska and Jesus Christ." There's no doubt in my mind this song is Nebraska's 15 minutes of fame.

Somewhere around the midway point, I rocked out to Train's Save Me San Francisco. The chorus of the song is my new marathon training mantra: "I've been high, I've been low, I've been yes and I've been oh hell no."

This is absolutely true. Some days are smokin' good, some I'd rather bury.

And the OH, HELL NO happens once a day, regardless.

A few paces further and I was using Midas's leash as a microphone, in the middle of the street no less, to hold a private concert singing Orianthi's According to You. If anyone noticed, I openly don't care.

On the home stretch, Kelly Clarkson's Catch My Breath had tears streaming down my face. Her words, "Laughing hard with the windows down. Leaving footprints all over town." That's how I feel. And when she croons, "Now that you know…this is my life. I won't be told what's supposed to be right," the bad-a** in me cries out, "Hell, yeah!"

HOLY CRIPES.

I'm not normally this emotional. I usually get up, put my big-girl pants on and methodically work my monster to-do list without much fanfare.

But this? Hooboy. This maniacal experience has me running through all sorts of feelings. (Think baggage, bull sh*t, fear, chaos, bliss, etc.) And yeah, I'm definitely running into crazy.

At this rate, I have no bloody idea who I'll be post-marathon. But I guaranfreakintee it won't be who I am today.

I secretly believe everyone has their own brand of crazy; it's kind of a new form of sisterhood.

Trash Talks

Wednesday is trash day in my neighborhood.

It's not that trash is sexy. But trash is *telling*.

I hesitated to share this because I detest gossip. I don't have stalker tendencies. This sh*t happens to me through osmosis. When you walk/run the same route(s) year after year, you tend to pick things up.

Here's what you can tell by someone's trash:

- They've decided to upgrade their Christmas decorations. They're throwing their old sh*t out.

- Someone filed for divorce. (His or her stuff — whoever moved out — is curbside.)

- Who shops at Costco. (The boxes are a dead giveaway.)

- If your kids eat a truckload of Cuties each week.

- Who is a borderline boozer.

Listen. If you lifted the lids on my trashcans you'd be freakin' appalled. But, now that I know that trash talks, I get all kinds of strategic on trash day. I want my secrets to stay my secrets.

Because I run the same route every morning, I'm also the first to know:

- Whose house went on the market.

- If you started a home improvement project.

- Who still has their f*ing Christmas tree up in their living room. Seriously people. It's four months past the holidays. That's just plain lazy.

- If the cops roll in to help stave off mayhem.

The cop bitty is new.

This morning, Midas and I are out in the fog chasing five miles. We're dodging Costo boxes and Cutie sacks left and right. He's snaggin' snacks at every driveway. We're pretty much keeping to ourselves, rockin' out to Cat Steven's Peace Train when the first cop car rolls by.

There were no flashing lights. It wasn't a high-speed chase. But last I checked, we don't have any cops who live in the neighborhood.

And I would know.

A few minutes later, cop car No. 2 rolls by. That's when the hair on the back of my neck stood up.

Part of me wanted to dive for the bushes, like what the f*? Are they here for me? I'm secretly racking my brain for recent indiscretions or criminal activity. I've got nothing. Or better yet, I tell myself, they've got nothing on me.

As Midas and I make our final ascent, I notice one of the cop cars parked quietly at the end of my street.

The other car is in front of my neighbor's house.

I feel surrounded.

I make a beeline for my garage, unhook Midas's gear, get his daytime necklace snapped into place and hurriedly turn out the lights.

I sneak to the end of the garage to see if I can "see" anything. My ears have morphed into antennae that would rival Verizon's strongest signal.

Nothing. Damn it.

I have no idea what went down in my 'hood this morning. I may never know.

But I can say with total authority I was the *first* to know.

Here's to trash that talks, tinsel town and telling secrets.

I have a hot date tonight with my local running store to buy new shoes. My ASICS have 600+ miles on them and they're beat to sh*t. They even have holes in the TOP – WTH?!?!?

Plan B? Get Dragged.

Training for a marathon has taken over my life.

It has infiltrated my friendships; it freakin' owns my weekends; has taken up all of my extra brain space; and has completely run roughshod over my relationship with Hubs.

Last night was date night.

Hubs and I try to go out for dinner once a week. I'm not sure if we do it to catch up or so we don't have to cook. Maybe both.

It began with an outing to the local running store. You can tell the weather's warming, the store was packed with soon-to-be trail hoggers, which is another way of saying I'll soon be sharing my trail with dozens of fair-weather tread-burners.

We both were on the hunt for new shoes. Brook: 1. Hubs: 0.

I inquired about a fix for wearing holes in the tops of my shoes. The clerk's reply? Duct tape. On the inside. Applied upside down to the top of your shoe.

Cripes almighty. I should have known. I duct tape my ear buds to my chest for hell's sake; it appears this sticky roll of gray goodness is the end-all-be-all solution for everything. You might be redneck...

But, I digress. Back to shoes: I opted for the ASICS Gel Nimbus 14 again. I'm such a chicken sh*t. This close to game day, I don't have time to figure out if another brand of shoe will shut me down, blow out my appendix or bruise my digits.

They're kind-of ugly. But if you're a runner, you know as well as I do that looks take a back seat to their "git-er-done" attitude.

I also snagged a flip belt. I won't spend any time here because I'll be returning this way-too-small-ride-up-to-your-boobs loop of spandex.

After laying down $200, we head to one of our favorite sushi restaurants.

Here's where I confess I'm a total fraud. I hate seafood. I think I'm allergic. So, I always opt for the avocado and teriyaki beef rolls. I don't want my Nebraska peeps to think I've gone all "big city."

Over dinner I say to Hubs, "I want an honest answer. Are you tired of hearing about all things marathon?" His reply: "I'm pretty saturated with it, yes."

He's an engineer. Can you tell?

I came back with, "Do you think I'll finish?" His response, "Hell, yes I think you'll finish. If I have to throw your a** on a skid plate and drag you behind my motorcycle across the finish line, I'll do it."

"Wouldn't that chew up the skin on my a**?" I croak. "It could possibly *melt* the skin on your a**," he smiles back.

So the pressure's off. I now have a Plan B.

Pushed, pulled or dragged …

I've got this.

Midas was uber pokey today. (Four miles.) Five years ago, we established a "No Man Left Behind" pact, so I was pokey right along with him. I know he's already repaid the favor hundreds of times.

Blow Your Own Damn Mind

If I could go back, I would do a number of things differently training for my FIRST marathon.

Getting a few more massages would definitely be one of them.

Before heading out for my massage yesterday, I did some quick research on whether or not massage benefits the recreational runner. It kind of irks me that I'm still considered an average Joe, but whatever.

The info I found was conflicting. Some experts say yes, massage is beneficial. Others say no, there's literally zero effect.

Seriously?! If you're training for anything, even a trip to the grocery store, buck the freakin' naysayers and hop up on that comfy table as often as your pocketbook allows.

Here's why I got a massage: I decided to chase 20 miles tomorrow.

A series of events this week shoved me toward this decision:

- I talked to my good friend and athletic trainer Andi. On the phone earlier this week she said, "Sister, time's up. Get out there and shake your a**. Screw 18 miles. I know you can do 20, go do it."

- Then, while chatting up my girlfriend Chris, I mentioned I was chewing on 20. I bemoaned that I didn't want to tell anyone. She came after me with a, "WTH? You've never kept anything from us. Why would you start now? We love you because you tell the freakin' truth."

- I texted D.R. and said, "I'm thinking 20 miles Saturday. You in? F* 18 miles. She hates me." D.R.'s response? "You betcha I am in. You're gonna tear that trail a new a-hole on Saturday."

- And finally, yesterday, a former client sent a quote out in her newsletter. It stopped me dead in my tracks.

"Once in a while, blow your own damn mind."

Those simple words lit my soul on fire.

It struck me that throughout this entire process, that's exactly what I've been doing. I am blowing my own damn mind.

With every step, every long run, (win or lose), every blog post, every question I ask and every truth I share.

It's so easy to watch other people do heroic sh*t and sit safely on the sidelines. But what if life was a series of mind-blowing events? What if we could wake up, blow our minds, take a nap, snag a cocktail (and a carb!), and do it again the next day and the next?

Hell yeah.

So, tomorrow I'm chasing 20. I've done what's mine to do to prepare. I'm bringing the heat, the stink, the tums and the saltines.

Everything I think I'll need to blow my mind and blow 20 miles out of the water.

Life looks pretty amazing from this view. It makes me think I'd like to blow my mind way more often.

Everything But My Pride

Day 77

I left everything but my pride out on the trail today.

My legs. Some tread. A few tears. My heart. My bloody hipbones. Some skin. My SOUL. Every f*ing thing I had in my "git-er-done" toolbox. Did I blow 20 miles out of the water? Absolutely not. Did I earn every last freakin' mile of my 20 mile run today? You bet your a** I did.

Here's how it went down:

I'm driving to the trailhead pretty freakin' excited about chasing my first big 2-0. I rested last night. Ate a ginormous bowl of pasta. Skipped the ice cream and the vodka. Chugged a half-a-bottle of probiotic. Packed saltines, tums, my old shoes, pants -- everything I thought I'd need to kill it today.

As I pulled into the parking lot, it crossed my mind I should probably be scared. F*ing terrified, actually.

All of my long runs have been full of adventure, bullsh*t and hard-won lessons. I usually manage to get through my short weekday runs without incident, but the long runs are another story. I had no idea what today would bring — but I knew it'd be something memorable.

I hooked up with D.R., gave her my bag of goodies, and off I went. It was chilly. The sun was starting to rise. The first seven miles were perfect.

In the middle is where sh*t got messy.

Around mile eight, I got the appendicitis cramp. And I thought, "No f*ing way. I'm not caving to this today." I walked between miles 8.5 and nine. D.R. and I meet at mile nine, thank God.

As I hobble toward her I cry out, "My shoes! I need my old shoes!" I wore my new treads today. Big mistake. So we switched inserts, retied the old treads and away I went. I then jogged/stumbled to the 10-mile mark.

As I turned around to head back, I went banging on God's door.

No way! Absolutely not! This isn't fair! I've worked my a** off for this. My legs and my lungs feel fantastic. This can't be freakin' happening to me. Again! Please! I've got miles to run. Peeps to tell. Sh*t to do. Can't we work something out?

On the trek back to D.R. I considered my options:

- Fold 'em. Again.

- Or walk/stumble/crawl all the way back to the starting line.

I knew my only option was to finish this b*tch.

I shared my plan with D.R. She said, "Baby girl, whatever it takes." So, I chow a handful of saltine crackers, pop open a sleeve of Clif Bloks, and push onward.

A quarter-mile down the trail I feel ready to try again. The pain has subsided enough that I begin to jog. I make it to mile 13, check in with D.R., and tell her I'm going to keep truckin'.

At this point I've had to change my stride significantly to compensate for the pain in my core. My arms were positioned closer to my chest. My steps were smaller. My eyes were glued to the ground. I'd have run hunchback to get this done, seriously.

I'm not going to tell you I didn't stop to walk a bit and stretch sh*t out. I did. With 5.38 miles left, I briefly looked up and thought, "Sh*t! I'm so focused on the trail I wouldn't know if Brad Pitt just ran by." Or Ryan Gosling, Hugh Jackman — anyone worth a peek for hell's sake.

The last two miles I started to feel human again.

I forced myself to look around. That's when I saw a zillion 21-year-old girls bouncing along the trail. They were in their super sexy short-shorts. They looked cute as sh*t. Worse yet, they were barely sweating.

And there I was in my CAT hat and winter gloves. My clothes were drenched with 18 freakin' miles of sweat. I wanted to cry out, "This is mile 19 girls! Take that! I'm f*ing awesome! I didn't fold, puke, die or quit! Who gives a damn that you look amazing, I am a warrior!" I kept my mouth shut. But don't kid yourself; it was hard.

The last 10th of a mile I began to cry.

I was officially burning down the finish line of my first ever 20 mile run. I was (and am!) proud of myself.

D.R. meets me at the end and hugs me until I stop sobbing.

I'm not kidding when I say I earned every single mile today. I left almost everything I had on that trail. The only thing I brought back was my pride.

And now I know: Pride is enough.

Midas and I had a heart-to-heart last night. I needed to let him know he wasn't going to leave the yard today. After a few minutes, he looks at me and said, "Yeah Mom. I hear you."

Borrowed Motivation

Day 78

After yesterday's 20-mile throw down, I needed some balm for my soul.

I took a nap. Then, I ate everything I could get my hands on. Literally, if it fit inside my mouth, I devoured it. (I wish I were kidding.) I trekked over to my neighbors, in my pajamas, no less, to guzzle a much-deserved cosmo. I also spent several hours reflecting on this crazy, soulful journey to 26.2.

Here's where my mind went:

- Why in the f* are my long runs loaded with drama?

- Do I have a chronic appendicitis? A hernia?

- Maybe I should find a reflexologist or an acupuncturist.

- Will this adventure kill me? (It won't; I'm dramatic.)

I also considered why I feel compelled to tell this story.

Hey, this is not the sexiest thing I've ever done. It's one of the best -- definitely one of the hardest -- but it's not like I run around looking all hot and sh*t. I mean, come on, nearly everyone I know has seen me at my worst -- not necessarily my idea of celebrity status.

Before I agreed to bust my a** chasing this dream, I read *The Non-Runner's Marathon Guide for Women* by Dawn Dais.

God bless, this woman is hilarious.

In the book, she gives a blow-by-blow of all things chaffing, gear, accessories, the lifestyle and the big day. She also covers everything sh*tty and hard about training. Many-a-time this lady rolled around on the ground during a long run cursing the Gods and begging for mercy.

(Note: If you are even considering a marathon, it's a must read. It's laugh-out-loud good.)

After I read the book, I thought, "Sh*t. If this lady can do a marathon, I can too. Hell, yeah. Count me in."

If I met her today, I'm not sure if I'd punch her in the mouth or ask for her autograph. Maybe both.

Here's where this gets a little deep: I believe women have a soul-level responsibility to support each other, offer encouragement, give a leg up, lend a hand, tell the truth, see each other as nothing less than powerful, courageous, bold and beautiful.

That said, I didn't start training for a marathon to inspire anyone other than my damn self.

But here are some of the notes I've received from people:

"You rock!!! You have also inspired me. I've run half's but never considered a marathon, but now I'm thinking of doing one! Keep on trucking on. You got this!"

+++++++++++++++++

"Go You! Congratulations! You're an inspiration! I'll be running my first marathon in October (the Chicago Marathon) and you are paving the way for me by helping me to understand what to expect. Thank you!"

+++++++++++++++++

"Awesome story! You are an inspiration, especially to someone like me who is just beginning a fitness journey! Thanks for sharing! Congrats and good luck on your next 20-miler!"

+++++++++++++++++

"Thought about you and your journey on my own 10-miler this morning. Got behind a girl sporting a shirt that read, "Never underestimate the strength of a woman," and it stuck with me throughout the race! Keep on truckin!"

+++++++++++++++++

"Going for my first 10-miler tomorrow. I'm inspired by your grit and determination! Carry on warrior!"

+++++++++++++++++

"Congratulations Brook!! You're an awesome, amazing lady; you have me motivated for my first marathon this fall. You story will definitely keep me going."

+++++++++++++++++

"You are an incredible finisher! I, too, had tears in my eyes for your finish! Wow. Have you motivated me to push past 5.68 miles? OMG!! Yes you have sole-sister! Yes, you have!

So here's the deal. If Dawn Dais can, then I can. If I can, then you can.

If you can, someone you know can, too.

Freakin' awesome how this works.

Today Midas and I walked a few miles. My feet are still p*ssed. Back in the saddle tomorrow.

Money = Motivation?

Money makes the world go 'round.

That doesn't mean it's a foolproof formula for full-on bliss, but I have yet to meet a person who doesn't need it or who doesn't want a tad bit more of it.

A few months ago, I mentioned my sister-in-law, Dannika, and I formed the $1K Club. How it works: Six women (including me) each wrote a check for $1,000. If we reach our individual goal within six months, we get our check back. If not, the check gets cashed and the winners split the pot.

Dannika and I thought we were brilliant forming this club. After all, it's a win-win.

If you take the weight off, or in my case run a marathon, you're a winner. You get your check back. Winner. You make a little extra money if someone's check gets cashed. Again, winner.

A few nights ago, we chatted about money as a motivator. I asked her if her $1,000 was motivating her to lose weight. Nope. I called my Mom, who is also a member. I asked if her $1,000 was motivation enough to reach her weight-loss goal. Nope. Then, I thought about every last bloody bit of bull sh*t I've been through to train for this marathon.

Would I run a marathon for $1,000? F* no.

Listen, when your brain loses contact with your legs and your hip bones start beggin' for mercy around mile 15, there is no amount of money in the world that would make you keep going if you didn't want to. I wouldn't run a marathon for a new car or a lifetime supply of Ben & Jerry's. True story.

We're not ditching the club. It will press on and so will we. But I find it fascinating that in this case, money hasn't been a motivator.

I wanted to know if the members of the $1K Club were the exception to the rule, so I went online in search of evidence that would support or debunk the theory that money motivates.

Some experts shared that yes, investing in your running can push you to train more consistently. One went so far as to recommend you pay yourself for every mile you run.

Seriously?! If paid myself a dollar for every mile I've run since January 1, I'd be in the freakin' poor house.

And about weight loss: According to a study published in The Journal of the American Medical Association in 2008, having a financial incentive to lose weight could make you five times more likely to succeed. Who knew?

Without question, my motivation for running a marathon has come from within. And I want this so dang much I'll do almost anything to get it.

FREE RESOURCE: In case you missed it, you can download the rules to set up your own $1K Club at www.MarathonTrainingTools.com. Five out of our six members reached their goal...awesome!

16 Bags of Pretzels

Hubs and I met on Match.com.

At the time, I lived in Wyoming. The only place you'll meet a guy in Wyoming is at the local bar or at church. And I guaranfreakintee he won't be under the age of 75. Hence, I had to take my search online.

I'm fairly certain somewhere in my online profile I said, "Loves to travel." I probably said a lot of stuff that may or may not be true. And back then, maybe I did like to travel. But nowadays, it seems like a heroic effort to get anywhere that requires a connecting flight.

Yesterday's trip to the East coast was painful.

I got to the Denver airport 90 minutes before my flight. I walked right up to the ticket counter and handed over all of my favorite clothes to an airline employee who looks likes she eats small children for breakfast.

Not one to be deterred by a sourpuss, I sail through security and snag a grilled chicken wrap at Mickey D's. I hate to admit I ate McDonalds, but damn it, I did.

Me + Travel + Hungry = Guaranteed Call to Security.

I get situated in seat 19C. I paid for an aisle seat upgrade. It's inevitable: When you're a party of one, the airline automatically stuffs you in the middle.

After all that effort, we end up sitting on the runway for 40 minutes before takeoff. Delta totally missed the boat by not offering free cocktails.

Because the flight was delayed, I had to bust a move to make my connection. As I'm hauling a** down the concourse, two thoughts run through my mind: 1) I have to pee and 2) I'm starving. I only had 3 minutes to get to the gate before they closed the door forever. I knew I had to choose. The reality is, my body chose for me. (I hit the restroom.)

I scoot down the jet way and throw myself into the cabin. I look one of the flight attendants dead in the eye and cry, "I'm freakin' *starving*. Do you have anything I can buy to stave off hunger and save the other passengers from my wrath?"

It's a 38-minute flight. There's no food or beverage service. She takes pity on me and stuffs 16 bags of pretzels and a Biscotti cookie in my purse. I'm no longer breaking up with Delta.

I land without further incident. I chased down a cab. It was a white, unmarked mini-van. The inside reeked of stale cigarettes. A few minutes into the ride, the driver rolled up the windows, locked the doors and said he had some groovy music to share. Oh sh*t.

We are zooming down some foreign-to-me-interstate listening to Star Castle. Their Fountains of Light album. It's 70s. Psychedelic. Awful. If you love them, forgive me. I'm more of an 80s girl, myself.

He was so proud of that album he insisted on showing me the CD cover. So, I feigned love and interest of all things Star Castle, which is probably how I made it to the hotel without being kidnapped. He asked if I wanted to schedule my return trip with him. Um, no.

Fifty dollars later, I walk into the hotel lobby and who do I see? The flight attendants from Delta. One of them looks at me and says, "Hey, you're that hungry girl from our flight. We were just laughing about you."

It's a small world. I'd best remember it behooves me to be nice.

Here are my lessons:

- One CLIF Bar in your purse simply isn't enough.

- Never get into an unmarked mini-van. No exceptions.

- Be nice to the airline peeps. They just might save your a**.

- Before you turn over gear to be placed in the belly of an airplane, consider what you'll do if you make it to your final destination and your bags don't. I thought about it. Honestly, I need a toothbrush and a fresh pair of drawers way more than I need running shoes.

And finally, when in doubt, feign love and interest of all things Star Castle.

A Trip To Crystal World

Yesterday, I shopped for crystals on my lunch break.

I know, right!? It wasn't my idea. A few colleagues asked if I wanted to tag along on their excursion to Crystal World. Never one to pass on an adventure I thought, why not? I'm mostly open to all things metaphysical: crystals, healers, psychics, energy work, etc. That said, don't tell my Mom. (She can barely stand when I skip church.)

When we walked in I thought I'd try the twitch test, which basically means you *feel* the energy of the stones to see if any respond to you. Yeah, right. Not one single pebble in that entire freakin' store wanted to be mine.

After fondling every stone I could get my hands on, I finally mustered the courage to ask if they had anything that could help with running. You know, something that could make you run faster. Be fearless. Live pain free. Run a marathon, effortlessly.

Stones that could take out heartburn with a single blow.

Nada.

I, then, inquired if they had anything to improve/support endurance. Ding! Ding! Ding!

They directed me to Moss Agate. Turns out, Moss Agate is extremely beneficial as a body strengthener in times of stress. (Who the f* is stressed?) It enhances mental concentration, persistence and endurance, making it useful as an aid in physical exercise programs, therapies, or body building.

It also brings friendships, new love, (sorry Hubs), and abundance. I'm freakin' all over that, especially for a whopping $1.50 per stone. I can afford to swallow the damn thing on race day if need be.

Sans my trip to crystal world, I sat inside all freakin' day. I had an f*ing headache that would rival Armageddon. Think: roaring, pounding and pulsing behind your eyes, awful. Around 5 p.m., I headed to my hotel room and changed into my fat man pants. I needed fresh air. A walk. Some tunes and an hour to clear my mind.

It was seriously the first time in a month I've been nowhere near my cell phone. The only way to describe it is bliss.

Near the end of my trek, I swung into the chocolate store. Good freakin' night. That store was bursting with sugar and sin -- everything I needed and deserved to win the war against my headache.

I picked up their Milk Chocolate Caramel Sea Salt treats. I bought four and proceeded to eat every last one of them.

For dinner, it was a stiff vodka tonic and the fattest rib eye the cooks in the kitchen could dig up. It's crazy how a killer piece of red meat and a mean cocktail can cure all of my ails.

Here are today's lessons:

- It's totally okay to shut sh*t off. Whatever "it" is for you. Your energy. Your cell phone. Your computer. Your TV. Every last blessed piece of technology you own. You'll find what you're looking for in the silence.

- Chocolate, vodka and red meat can cure anything.

- When you're training for a marathon, you can leave your high heels at home. There ain't no way your dawgs will let you wear them.

- Stay open to anything. I named my new pet rock Mossy. I am either borderline crazy or f*ing brilliant.

I spend most of my time tearing through life and then circling back to tell the story.

But the truth is, there's no story to tell unless you actually *live* life first.

Someone in my meeting said my next adventure (post-marathon) should be private labeled vodka. What do you think?!

Runners Do That?

Two other people rocked the road with me this morning.

Kwavi is a marathoner from Atlanta; Jack, also from Atlanta, just ran a relay marathon in Knoxville. The three of us have known each other for about six months. (We happen to be in the same business mastermind group.)

We hooked up in the lobby of our hotel at 5 a.m. and headed out for a 4.5-mile run. We left our footprints all over town.

We used our time together to catch up on partners, kids, dogs, and of course, all things running.

Listen. I have only run with one other person once in my life. So I've never tried to carry on a conversation while running. Sweet mother of pearl. Talking and running at the same time is an entirely different form of exercise. I learned super-quick to keep my f*ing mouth shut on the hills.

None of us are strangers to rockin' the road. That said, our experiences are enormously different.

I asked Kwavi about her first marathon. (She did the Chicago last year.) We talked about the energy, the sheer volume of people and the chaos. That's when she busted out that some runners wear Depends undergarments on race day so they don't have to stop and pee.

Or sh*t.

WTF?!?! I was like, "No Way! You can't possibly sh*t while you're running. Or can you? Even if you could, who would do that?" I thought for sure she was pulling my leg.

Jack backed her up.

People. Don't. Freakin'. Do That. No race is worth sh*tting your pants for. Come on.

Then, I shared a story I heard while chatting with another marathoner. Apparently, some races are so big they can't possibly have enough port-a-potties to go 'round. So they lay tarps on the ground. Runners drop their britches, squat and do whatever it is they need to do. No. 1 or No. 2. Anything goes.

Hey, if you've peed on a tarp, I'm cheering for you. I'd do the same damn thing if I was desperate. But there is no amount of money in the world that would have me doing anything else.

You had to know bathroom business would find its way into this conversation. I've only talked about it once is 84 days. Back then, I didn't know enough to ask the right questions. It's kind of terrible, very freakin' funny and absolutely good to know.

We made it back to the hotel full of smiles and first-rate mojo.

Just before we parted ways, I told Kwavi I brushed my chicklets this morning as I knew I'd have companions. She laughed and shared, "I thought about you as I was brushing my teeth this morning. I know you usually don't, and sister, there's no way I'm not brushing mine."

Her comment made me think about all I've shared about marathon training. Sometimes too much. But I think we can learn from each other. And you don't know what you don't know, right?

So today, I'm celebrating sharing, smiles and way more than I wanted to know about sh*t.

Jack is the first person EVER to tell me I am funny. (I had no idea.) Thank God he told me that before I started this journey. Can you image reading boring, dry, awful monologues about training for a marathon? Even my BFF would bail on that gig. So thanks, Jack, for making this entire adventure laughable.

Top 5 Mistakes

I've spent two years climbing the proverbial running ladder.

Two short years ago, I laid down my first-ever 5k. A year later, it was a 5-miler. Then, I ran my first 10k, which for me was a damn big deal.

After the 10k, I got way more serious about training/running. I went from interested to I'm all kinds of in on this.

Last fall, I finished two half marathons.

With all these runs under my belt, I still consider myself a baby.

I'm the first to admit I rolled into marathon training without knowing nearly enough. (Whatever the f* "enough" means.) In hindsight, I've made some fairly ridiculous, somewhat reckless, uber messy mistakes. And hey, who doesn't like reading about other people's mistakes?!

Before you read on, I want to note that these are my Top Five mistakes — not all of my mistakes, mind you. Stand by, it shouldn't take me too long to burn my a** or my pocketbook on a few more.

BK's Top Five Marathon Training Mistakes

1) Training Schedule.

My training schedule is far too long. (And I'm not just sayin' this because I'm f*ing over long runs.) I started with a half marathon base. My schedule should have been four months, not five. I've probably over-trained, a little. No doubt the Type A, highly structured, borderline anal part of me is to blame.

2) Cross Training.

I would have incorporated a lot more cross training (CT). Other forms of exercise would have built my total body strength and conditioning, which would have made me a stronger, better runner. Right now, I can crank out the miles, but CT would have made me faster. Toner. Fitter. Definitely hotter.

3) Nutrition.

I'd have hired a nutritionist day one to create a customized meal plan. Hands down my biggest challenge has been food. No one teaches you how to fuel your body instead of stuff your face. The investment here would have saved me time, money and heartache. Maybe heartburn, too.

4) Support/Guidance.

Listen. No one tells you how to run your first marathon. You have to figure out far too much sh*t on your own. I've wasted time, money and my joints making some expensive and painful mistakes. I think I'll write a survival guide when my first marathon is done. It will be loaded with cuss words and truths.

5) Measurements/Metrics.

This sounds lame, but I'd have measured and tracked every stinkin' body part I could get a tape around. I definitely would have tracked my weight and body fat. If you're going to commit five months of your life to something, I believe the numbers will keep you motivated.

I've made a sh*t load of mistakes; these are just my Top five to-date. If you asked me to freakin' list 100, there's no doubt I could. But Sophia Loren says it best: "Mistakes are part of the dues one pays for a full life."

And that's exactly what I'm chasing.

Travel sucks: $4 for a freakin' water. There had better be some anti-aging properties hidden in that bottle.

FREE RESOURCE: If you haven't yet downloaded your free Measurement Mastery Worksheet, get instant access at www.MarathonTrainingTools.com.

Itty Bitty Sh*tty Committee

My girlfriend Andi and I put up 18 miles today.

Neither of us kicked out a personal best. Andi complained that her legs felt sluggish. And of course, my f*ing appendicitis side-stitch kicked into high gear around mile 11. F*.

I haven't had a solid long run in a month. That's four long weeks of weak, painful, defeating runs. Between heartburn, nearly puking and the cramps in my side, I've had a sh*t go of things.

But, we finished strong all things considered. Eighteen miles in 3:30, which included a pit stop and a bit of walking/stretching. The good news is, if I can get my side cramp figured out I might just finish the marathon in 4:30.

My lessons today are few, but they're enormous:

Lesson No. 1 - If you don't take care of your body, it can't possibly take care of you. I've asked mine to perform heroic acts since I started training, yet I've refused to make time to see the doctor. WTF? The only person I have to blame is myself. And I'm f*ing p*ssed.

I can fly all over the country; serve my clients; see friends; feed the dog; carry out the most mundane of tasks; eat well; skip the vodka; pass on ice cream; spend money on chiropractic, massage, new shoes and a support person. But I have yet to pick up the phone to make a measly freakin' doctor's appointment. Christ.

During one of my meetings last week, health was an uber hot topic. The gist was entrepreneurs often trade their health for the health of their bottom line. Then, they wonder why they're forced to sit sh*t out and recover from XYZ. During the conversation, someone bellowed out:

You have to stop putting sh*t in your shrine. (Note: A shrine is your body.)

In that moment, I thought about my struggle with food and nutrition during marathon training: cinnamon rolls, Cheetos, binge eating, heartburn, ways to eat on the run, what to eat, when to eat ... you catch my drift.

But today, I realized food and nutrition are only part of the equation.

You have to care for your shrine on every level. Trust me, your body, mind and spirit leave you no freakin' choice anyway, so don't bother fighting.

For me, this means:

- Fueling my body to perform to the best of its ability.

- Protecting my confidence that I can and will get this done.

- Setting up doable systems (like training!) that make sense and work for me.

- Surrounding myself with people who believe I can do this.

- Putting my physical health first – and making a bleepity bleep, bleep, bleep doctor's appointment.

The truth is, I'm scared. I'm sure it's nothing, but I don't know if I want to know something's wrong. I'm only five short weeks from the marathon, which isn't a lot of time to figure sh*t out.

So I have two choices.

- Do nothing and hope for the best.

- Find out what's up and see if I can squeeze in a few killer long runs before D-day.

For me, hope is not a strategy. That'd be like hoping you can run 26.2 with no training and a brown bag on your head. Yeah, right. So I'm calling the doctor Monday.

Lesson No. 2: Know when enough is enough.

There was a time not too long ago when 18 miles was nowhere on my radar. I've trained for weeks and weeks and weeks to lay the big boys down. (I.e., 18 and 20 miles.)

Today, my itty bitty sh*tty committee screamed that 18 miles wasn't enough. "You should go for 20! Doing just 18 is lazy! It's the joker's way out! You're quitting! Push on! Who cares if there's a knife in your side? Anything less than 20 is total failure!"

On the drive home, I chewed on my committee's harsh words. Here's where I shook out:

F* that. Doing 18 miles is epic.

And today, it was more than enough.

I stopped by my magical P.O. Box on the way home from the airport yesterday. My friend Laura sent a fabulous piece of sole sister jewelry. It's perfect.

15 Minute Pity Party

Last night I spent a good 15 minutes feeling sorry for myself.

My side hurt. I got out of the tub and realized my sports bra had left chafe marks on my freakin' back. Seriously?! I also have some nasty bug bites on my left shoulder that itch to high hell and are ugly as sin. Overall, I was feeling beat to sh*t.

I went and sat next to Hubs and asked if he'd take part in my, "Lets feel sorry for me" party. He refused, damn it.

The good news is my sour mood didn't last long. I considered all of the truly cool sh*t that's playing out in my life right now. And I realized that when I started saying YES! to life, life started saying YES! to me.

For example: Last night I made a new friend named Christy.

A few months ago, she found me via Facebook. She's been a faithful blog reader and a really big fan of my crazy a** journey. A few weeks ago, she emailed me to share her personal story and to thank me for sharing mine. She said she'd be in Denver in April and asked if I'd be available to meet.

Normally, I would have blown this off. I value my weekends and it takes an act of God and Congress to get my a** off the couch on a Saturday night. But I said yes, and I'm so glad I did.

The same thing happened Friday flying home from the east coast.

To escape the stale-cigarette-smelling-Star-Castle-loving-joy-ride-taxi, I said YES! to hiring a car service to deliver me, unscathed, back to the airport.

My driver was Robert Lee, who happens to be the undefeated Tri-State Area Kick Boxing Champion.

For 30 minutes, he blasted me with weight lifting and cross training tips. He shared simple things I could do to become a better runner. Robert has knocked out more people in the first round than I have pairs of shoes.

Not only that, but he called me Boss Lady at least 17 times. I loved him at hello.

At the airport check-in counter, I was told my flight had been cancelled, which meant I had three long, lonely hours to kill. To add to the chaos, all of their credit card machines were down.

I don't know about you, but I never carry cash, which means I was stuck in the airport with no way to buy a coffee, breakfast or a measly bottle of water. This is a scary place to be when you're training for a marathon.

Enter Wendy.

Wendy, who I've never met before in my life, walked up and handed me a $10 bill. She said, "Go get yourself some breakfast." I looked at her in total disbelief. When my brain came back online I called out, "Wait! Can I write you a check for this?" She smiled and came back with, "Pay it forward."

When we finally boarded, I ended up next to a plastic surgeon from Jacksonville.

Let me tell you, nothing will make you more self-conscious than sitting next to someone who makes people beautiful for a living. I was all kinds of irked that he was sitting on my bad side.

We laughed our a**es off all the way to Atlanta. I swear to you my lips were rolled back and stuck to my front teeth the entire flight. I had tears streaming down my face.

Then yesterday, Carrie, who is part of the Facebook tribe, posted a photo along with this note:

"You don't know us but after your tarp blog we were intrigued. Look what we found at the Ukrops 10k in Richmond? However, it wasn't for the poops; it was just for meeting up with friends, which made people look twice when we posed for the photo. I'll keep my eyes peeled at future races."

Now you see why I can only feel sorry for myself for 15 minutes.

I haven't laughed this much in my entire life. I've met cool new peeps and picked up a few helpful tips. People are literally throwing money at me. They're also poop posing on tarps. (Talk about being all-in!)

Who knew training for a marathon could be so damn much fun?

Breaking Of The Glass

I attended my first Jewish wedding last night.

The ceremony was unlike anything I have ever witnessed. I grew up Lutheran; we don't have quite as many theatrics or rituals, which is a total bummer.

The bride walked around the groom 7 times during the ceremony. It was a sight to behold considering her dress weighed 70 pounds. The Rabbi sang tunes in Hebrew, which might as well have been in tongues. I so wasn't following. At the end of the service, the bride broke the glass and we all shouted, "Mazel Tov!"

There's something very liberating and downright awesome about shouting at a wedding. I may start crashing Jewish weddings just to keep my shout-out muscles in shape.

Breaking of the glass has numerous meanings.

Here's the one I like best: A broken Jewish wedding glass is forever changed; likewise, the couple are forever changed by the marriage and take on a new form.

Not to be lame, but I kind of feel that way about training for a marathon.

When you train for your first, you are forever changed. You do take on a new form. You become someone you never knew you could be.

Today, I own more running shoes than sassy shoes. My preferred headdress of choice is a freakin' Caterpillar stocking cap. I spend hours every Saturday dripping sweat in public. I wear the rattiest pair of ancient long underwear known to man. The best part about all of this is I just plain don't care what anyone else thinks. I care what I think.

Last night's festivities got me thinking: How do I want to celebrate burning down my first 26.2?

- I will definitely break one of my wine glasses in the driveway. I may even shout Mazel Tov! What the hell.

- Part of me wants to throw the doors of my house wide open and invite the world over to celebrate.

- The other part wants to leave the afternoon open for two margaritas and a fat four-hour nap.

While I don't yet have any concrete plans post-marathon, I have been thinking about what I'd like to do during the race, too.

I'm thinking of wearing a t-shirt that says: "Hi my name is Brook. It's my first marathon. Push." That or..."Hey, my name is Brook. Stand back. I'm bat sh*t f*ing crazy."

I'd also like to wear arm warmers with 13 names embroidered on each arm. The theory is you run one mile for each person, pet or cause you care deeply about. If I do this, Midas will be mile 24, Jesus snags 25 and I will be 26.

I met a guy at the wedding who has run eight marathons. His first took him five hours; his last took only 3:20. His advice for me: 1) Don't zoom through the start line looking for space in front of the pack; lock in your pace early; 2) Don't run for time on your first marathon. Run for *you.*

That's the plan.

During the dance last night, they lifted the bride and groom in their chairs and carried them around the dance floor. I'm considering putting an ad on Craigslist this week to find a team of peeps who would do the same for me at the finish line.

Moved To Silence

For 86 days I've had plenty to say about marathons.

Yesterday, I was moved to silence.

I'm still reeling from the news of the tragic events at the Boston Marathon. I thought about not blogging today, but it felt like a coward's way out. I've been 1000 percent transparent with you for the last three months. Why stop now?

After hearing the news, I immediately went to a place of fear.

Should I be worried? Will this happen again? Could it happen in Denver? Who does something like this? Will they catch them? Should I bail on my race? Will it ever be safe to run in public again?

On top of fear, I added devastation.

People lost their lives chasing or witnessing a dream yesterday. Over 150 were injured. As a runner, I can safely say bombs have never been on my radar. Unfortunately, for many of us, they will now be top-of-mind. I sincerely hope the innocence of running hasn't been irreversibly shattered.

Then, I stirred in some P*SSED OFF.

Running a marathon, whether it's your first or your 50th, is a big deal. Who the f* intentionally sets out to kill people, especially at a marathon? Whoever did this is a no-good-piece-of-sh*t-weak-gutless-a**hole.

But, there are still heroes in the world.

It didn't take long for national news to zoom in on the other runners, volunteers and law enforcement officials who ran *toward* the mayhem. It's easy to go to the place of, "Our world is a total sh*t storm." That said, I'm inspired to know there are still people who will risk their lives to assist others.

Here's where I've settled:

On the treadmill this morning, I refused to watch the news. I chose to start my day with my agenda, not the agenda of people who orchestrate catastrophes. Instead, I opened my heart and sent love, prayers and healing energy to my fellow runners and the entire city of Boston.

One of the reasons I decided to train for a marathon was to heal the fear in my life. Fear of commitment. Fear of failure. Fear of not being good enough. Fear of being out of control.

So I'll be damned if I'm going to get scared now.

I'm going to run my race. I hope you will run yours, too.

And as we cross the finish line, let's agree to have a moment to silence for those affected by yesterday's tragic events.

As our hearts break, we know your spirits are strong and mighty. We send love, health, healing, compassion and heart-felt prayers your way. XOXO.

Yesterday started what I hope will be my fast track to fabulous.

I finally mustered the courage to make a doctor's appointment to see what's up with my side cramp. I've got 31 days to figure sh*t out. Fingers crossed for miracles.

Shortly after I arrive at the medical clinic, I'm ushered to the patient room and the nurse asks why I'm there. I tell her I'm training for my first marathon and that I have crippling pain in my lower right quadrant.

Turns out, she's running the relay marathon at the same race. I'm telling you, sole sisters are everywhere. The good news is runners are taking over the world. No better people to be in charge in my book.

She takes my blood pressure – 110/70. BOOM.

Then, she tells me I have to unbutton my pants. ACK!

Girls, you know how it is when you go to the doctor. You always wonder if they'll have to go "there" to cure you.

I wait, with my pants unbuttoned, for 15 minutes. There's something very terrible about your pooch hanging through your pants for what seems to be eons, while you wonder if you'll have to take your pants all the way off.

In comes Dr. Walker. I'm disturbed she looks 16. I'm also a little jealous but WTH. "How long have you been practicing?" I croak. "Two years," she smiles.

She's probably been asked that 34 times a day for the last two years. I wanted to ask her age, but I was a tad worried my mouth would lead my a** to a lawsuit.

As we chatted, I tell her I'm training for a marathon. Turns out she's a marathoner herself. In that moment, my comfort level increased dramatically, which is totally lame. Running a marathon probably doesn't make you a better doctor.

I confessed to self-diagnosing on WebMd.com.

I run down the list of all the things that might be wrong with me. A sports hernia. Chronic appendicitis. Kidney infection. Intestinal pandemonium. Blah, blah, blah. Then, I realize I've probably insulted her.

I quickly apologize. She says with a raised brow, "No worries. People do it all the time."

She walks me through what she thinks might be wrong. It's probably not too serious as the pain isn't acute until around mile 10. She then orders blood tests, pee tests and abdominal, pelvis and trans-vaginal ultrasounds. Oh f*.

*At that point, the only thing going through my mind was how much is my f*ing deductible? I'll likely go broke finding the cure that allows me to kill my damn self chasing 26.2. This so wasn't in the cards.*

She asks if I understand what trans-vaginal means. I think she's joking, but I say yes. She proceeds to tell me, in fairly graphic detail, what to expect. Yes, it is a test where your pants have to come off. Sh*t.

I then head over to the lab and spurt out enough blood to fill 8,000 viles. Next up? Two pee tests. Within minutes, I'm driving home feeling a little deflated and very depleted.

As I'm responding to other people's agendas, an e-mail pops up that declares,

"TEST RESULTS ARE AVAILABLE."

And I think to myself, "Oh f*. They're going to tell me I'm *dying* in an e-mail." It takes me 30 minutes to talk myself in to viewing the results. It takes another 30 minutes to find my f*ing username and password to log on to the site.

I log in only to learn I'm not pregnant. I didn't even know they were doing a pregnancy test. I should ask more questions.

The good news is I'm not, yet, dying, which means I'm one step closer to burning down 26.2 pain free.

All of my ultrasounds are next week. You have to fast beforehand. Brook + No food = WAR. They have no idea what they're in for. I probably don't either.

It Takes A Team

Up until a few years ago, I was fiercely independent.

I rarely, if ever, asked for help. I told myself if I did ask I'd be seen as weak. Lame. Incompetent. Ridiculous. So, I constantly bucked the support, wisdom and encouragement of others thinking that I was the only person who would have my back. (So, so stupid.)

Recently, I've discovered there are people in the world willing to hold your hand, kick your a** or simply offer their cheering services because they can. I know, crazy, right?

Training for my first marathon, I've taken the full-on-shameless-I'd-love-to-have-your-help approach. (Note: Hubs thinks I'm grandstanding a bit, but he's an engineer so his opinion doesn't count.)

Most runners I meet train without much ado. They're up at 4 a.m. to squeeze in their run so they're back in time to get their kids off to school. They carry their own water on long runs. (This is heroic considering how much you have to carry.) They keep their stories, worries, fears, challenges and victories to themselves.

They learn about nutrition, gear, training, injuries and staying motivated the hard way -- through experience.

If this is your approach, kudos to you. I respect you for it.

But for me, I say f* that.

When I began training, I didn't think to myself, "Woo f*ing hoo! Who can I get carry my water? Who will I call when sh*t hits the fan? How many people will I need on my team to lay down 26.2 successfully?"

Four months ago, I didn't know enough to ask these questions. I can't even claim I know everything now.

But I can say with total conviction that the best thing I've done is surround myself with a team of people, friends, peers and professionals, who will do anything they can to help me reach my goal.

I have essentially, and somewhat unknowingly, built an Esteem Team.

I have a Saturday morning support person, a chiropractor, a massage therapist and now a medical doctor on my team. Obviously, I pay these people, but who cares?! Each of them brings their genius work to the table, which I value tremendously.

Then, there are my girlfriends. The sisters I call when I spin out, sh*t the bed, damn near barf trailside or kill my first 18 mile run.

And most importantly, there's YOU.

I wish I could share the notes I get from women all over the U.S. who are overcoming more bull sh*t than I could ever imagine to get out and rock the road.

Things like divorce, death, sickness, physical challenges, kiddo issues, men issues, fear, heartache, self-doubt. The list goes on, but you catch my drift.

To you I say, "You are simply amazing."

You have played a non-negotiable-uber-important-leading-role on my team.

Your kind words, acts of courage, strong-will, tenacity and determination have propelled me toward my finish line. They've also kept me telling this story, even when it's hard, weird or embarrassing to share.

Today, I'm celebrating the fact that you've got my back.

And I want you to know, I've got yours, too.

Midas is going to the vet today for his annual checkup. A few months ago, he weighed 102. I'm hoping for 95 today. I feel like I've been starving him.

Only One To Blame

I've been Midas's mama for five years.

He's my first dog. I'm always overwhelmed and surprised by how much I dig him. Who knew you could love an animal like a child?

When he was 10 weeks old, we started taking short walks around the neighborhood. Over time, we worked our way up to a few miles a day. Eighteen months ago, we began running together. (Think two miles, nothing outrageous.) Now, he wakes me up at 4:30 a.m., six days a week, to put up anywhere between three to five miles.

To see him, you'd think he is an innocent, blameless, well-behaved dog. Yeah, freakin' right.

Midas eats, on average, six rolls of toilet paper per week. He gets a biting case of the zoomies every night around 6 p.m. Without exception, he shreds every last toy he's gifted. At doggy daycare, they barely let him participate in "group play" for fear he'll annihilate another dog. We checked him in to a 30-day behavioral boot camp and he's still an a** hole.

There's not much left to do except love him.

Yesterday was his annual checkup.

If you have a dog, you know the first thing they do is put your beloved four-legged friend on the scale. Hooboy.

Midas has gained weight. And not just a little.

We've been fighting his weight for months. Sixty days ago, when they thought he had a thyroid problem, I cut his food intake significantly. Not only that, but for the love of all things holy, his amount of daily exercise is off-the-f*ing-charts. How can he be gaining weight? Don't they know he's training for a marathon?

He tipped the scales at 106 pounds. Holy Cripes.

Enter our Vet Dr. Downie. (P.S. – She's a sole sister, too; it helps!)

She walked in, and I could tell by the look on her face that Midas is B-I-G. (Think brows raised, eyeballs bulging.) And in this case, there's only one person to blame.

His mama.

I offered up every reason and excuse for his continued weight gain. I feigned ignorance. Then outrage. I blamed his food. His treats. His age. I'm telling you, I pulled out all the freakin' stops and delivered a full-blown production of Jekyll and Hyde right there in her office.

Worn out by my theatrics, the doc and I got down to business about his caloric intake, the table scraps I've been sneaking him, and possible next steps. Turns out they have a "doggie dietician" he'll be seeing in the near future.

Psst -- don't tell him he's on a diet; he'll be pissed.

Midas is my No. 1 go to I-love-you-even-when-you're-ugly road rockin' companion.

He's my alarm clock. He drags my sluggish a** up every hill in the neighborhood. He gives me plenty of opportunities to stop along the way while he sniffs sh*t out. Literally. There were many-a-morning I would have stayed in bed if it weren't for his wet nose bludgeoning my elbow.

There's something very honest about running with a dog.

He's always happy. He never quits. He couldn't care less about how many calories he burns (obviously) or how far we go. The only thing he cares about is high-tailing it out of the yard to chase down what the "bigger" world has in store for him.

We should all be so lucky.

*All of my test results sans the ultrasounds are back. The doc says I'm in awesome shape. The chiro this morning also said, "You're so much stronger than you used to be." Nice to know busting your a** leads to some killer outcomes.*

20 Miles? Hell, Yes.

I had the best run of my ever lovin' life today.

My training schedule told me I was up for 14 miles. Considering the last four long runs have been somewhat of a sh*t storm, I was hopeful, at best, that I'd knock out 14 with zero drama.

All week I'd been chewing on the reality that I may not run a marathon.

Don't get me wrong, I'm going to cross that f*ing finish line if I have to walk, crawl or be dragged. I've committed four full months of my life to this. I'm in way too deep to bail now. But based on my recent track record, I knew I'd likely be walking several miles of my 26.2.

Dr. Walker called yesterday to go over my test results. To paraphrase, she said, "You have some of the best results I've ever seen, and we tested for everything. I don't think we're going to find anything on the ultrasounds either."

I mirrored her sentiments.

Immediately, I went to a place of pain management. (It scares me I even know what that freakin' means. I watch way too much House.) I asked about IVs and/or pain pills on or before race day.

Note: After our conversation, who knows what she thinks of me. Maybe that I'm an addict. Maybe I should be.

She said, "No way," to pain pills.

1. They would make me tired.

2. I wouldn't be able to tell if something else was wrong.

3. It's anybody's guess what they would do to my stomach.

As I'm somewhat terrified of puking or sh*tting my pants on race day, it was difficult to argue.

So I asked, "Pending nothing comes back on the ultrasounds, what are my options?"

Her answer?

Ibuprofen.

You've got to be f*ing kidding. There's a small part of me that's outraged something as simple as ibuprofen may be the solution. I should have thought of that myself. But another part of me will be damn thankful if nothing is seriously wrong.

I also decided to chat up my sister-in-law yesterday. (The co-founder of the $1K Club.) I wanted to let her know I may not actually *run* a marathon. As I'm less than 30 days out; I thought it wise to be honest.

She exclaimed, "Good freakin' night. You've already run 20. This adventure has taken over your life. You've put in more work than anyone I know. Who gives a sh*t if you walk part of the race?" What a great sister-in-law.

So this morning, I was driving to meet D.R. and I was feeling scared, tired and deflated. I was positive I was going to have my a** handed to me on the trail. Again.

Listen. When you have less-than-solid long runs week after week, you start to question if you should even be doing this. I am sick of knowing my legs and lungs can run a marathon, but my side refuses to get in the f*ing game. I feel like one of those cartoon characters who runs face first into a brick wall, falls down, gets up and runs into the wall again. And again. And again. And again.

I would never bail; but don't kid yourself. My spirit was fatigued. Until today.

Before I left the house, I swallowed four ibuprofen. (Please don't write to me and say I'm wrecking my kidneys. I had to know if it would work.) I also ate some saltine crackers to stave off heartburn.

Andi, D.R. and I met-up uber early for the hand off. We head out seven miles. At 5.5 the cramp takes a few good swings at me. I don't stop. I do everything in my power to breathe through it.

Sh*t was dicey, at best, until the turn around at mile seven.

I made it all the way to 14 with no further trouble. A miracle.

I looked at Andi and said, "Girl, bail if you want to. I feel great. I've got to keep going." So we turned around and did one mile out and one mile back. I was at 16 miles.

Andi asked, "Again?" I say, "Absofreakinlutely."

We went out two miles and back. I was at 20. I felt freakin' amazing.

I looked at Andi and wondered aloud, "Should we go for 22?" She raised her brow and said, "Save 22 for a special day." So I did.

Afterwards, we guzzled chocolate milk like kids. I haven't had chocolate milk for at least 20 years, maybe more. It was so much better than I remembered.

Here are today's lessons:

- Be flexible on your training schedule. Get while the gettin' is good. Not every long run will be a win, so when you're in the zone, leave it all out on the trail.

- Don't quit. You never know when you'll come back and kill a long run. If you have a few sh*t experiences, press on. You won't know what you're capable of if you refuse to try.

I'm so freakin' thankful today worked out famously. I needed it; so did my confidence.

I'm back in the game and I'm ALL IN.

There's only one thing left to say…and today…it's perfect.

ONWARD!

Thank you for being with me on this ride. I love you more than you could possibly know. I'm off to have a margarita. I'm raising my glass to you. XO

What's Next?

I love the day after a long run.

Sans the fact I feel beat to sh*t, of course.

The day after is generally a Sunday, which means I sleep until at least 5:30 a.m. I don't have to rush around and get ready for the day. I chew on yesterday's run -- what worked and what didn't -- over a ginormous cup of coffee loaded to the gills with hot chocolate. I also spend time reflecting on the past week and what the next week holds.

In my case, the approaching week brings a few pesky ultrasounds and my first 22-mile throw down, which also happens to be my last monster run before race day.

In 29 days, I'll be standing at the starting line of my first full marathon. God willing, I'll cross the finish line on that same day.

With race day looming, lots of people are starting to ask, "Hey Brook, what's next?" (F* if I know.)

I'm not going to lie: My next steps have been heavy on my mind for the last few weeks. So, this morning I pulled out my journal to see if it could offer any insights. Inside, I re-read a letter I wrote to myself on my last birthday.

I wrote the letter pretending it was one year to the day later, and I looked back over the past 12 months. I wrote down everything I accomplished financially, physically, in relationships, in my business, etc.

Here's a peek at what's inside:

- You turned 37 today and the year has been a fun, fabulous, almost unbelievable ride. You ran two full marathons and you feel strong, fit and lean. (This leads me to believe I have another marathon in me.)

- You got another puppy. Midas loves him and it's been a smooth transition. (I don't know if this one will shake out. For hells sakes, I can hardly manage one dog, and I'm not sure I can afford to lose 12 rolls of toilet paper per week.)

- Katy bar the f*ing door – your business is soaring! You're working with your ideal clients and they get amazing results. You've added staff and you're in a location downtown on Blake Street.

- You live each day with a gratitude you've not known before. You're living the life you wanted to create for yourself and it looks damn good on you!

I closed the letter with: There's no end in sight. You've got this. Stay strong. Stay healthy. Keep going when you want to quit. Do your best. Be thankful. Help others. Use your voice. Love the journey. Be who you are meant to be on this planet so others are empowered to do the same. I love you. Be good, sister.

I wrote this before I decided to train for a marathon. Surprisingly, it all still applies.

Over the last 18 months, I've been checking sh*t off my bucket list with a vengeance.

1. Attend Richard Petty Driving School. Check.

2. Get my motorcycle's license. Check.

3. Join a high-level mastermind group. Check.

4. Run a marathon. (Damn near check.) This means it's probably time to add a few more items to the list.

As of today, I feel a tad bit torn.

On one hand, I've been tempted to call my psychic to see if she can reveal what my post-marathon life holds. Will I run another race? Chase another type of adventure? Go back to my old life? Help others run their first marathon, too? On the other hand, a big part of me is attached to the magic each day brings.

*When I decided to blog about this crazy a** adventure, I had no idea what would unfold. This journey has required me to be present in my life in a way that's both foreign and mystical; it's been good for me.*

So do I know what's next? Nope. Do I think the answers will come? Yep. If I've learned nothing else, I now trust, explicitly, that a power much greater than myself has my proverbial back. And honestly? The rest is just details.

14 Hours in Honolulu

I've spent a ton of time researching marathon stats.

As I'm en route to joining this elite group of peeps, I've been wondering if I'm the norm or the exception to all of their rules and averages. I've also been curious about how many people finish a marathon each year, which races are the biggest, the fastest times, average age, etc.

My online investigation netted some fairly cool findings:

- In 1990, there were 143,000 marathon finishers. In 2011, that number increased to 518,000. Even more amazing, half-marathon finishers grew from 482,000 to over 1.6 million. (See? Runners are taking over the world.)

- According to USARunning.org, the average age of a female long distance runner is 39. (I'm younger, but barely.) 62 percent are married; (Check!) 79 percent have a college degree; 42 percent have a post graduate degree (check!).

- Favorite race distances for women are: Half-marathon, 5k and 10k. (Hell yes, now I know why.)

Here are a few more fascinating factoids:

- The total percent of the U.S. population that has run a marathon: 0.5 percent.

- The record time for the fastest marathon ever run: 2:03.23. (Good freakin' night. I don't run a half-marathon in that time. Think sub five minute miles – wowzers.)

- There are 570 marathons held in the U.S. annually.

- Total fee for the New York City Marathon: $255.

- The average cost to run a marathon: $67. (This must be the average entry fee 'cause there ain't a person on the planet training for a marathon for 67 freakin' dollars.)

- Average number of sneakers a marathon runner goes through during training: 2. (I call B.S. Men must have lowered the average.)

- Average number of calories a woman burns during a marathon: 2,880. (I think this should be 25,000, but no one asked me.)

- Average number of miles ran per week during marathon training: 40. (Sweet Mother of Pearl.)

Here are the Top Five Largest U.S. Marathons:

1. New York City Marathon: 46,536 finishers

2. Chicago Marathon: 35,670 finishers

3. Boston Marathon: 23,879 finishers

4. Marine Corps Marathon: 20,895 finishers

5. L.A. Marathon: 19,626 finishers

In 2011, posted marathon times in the U.S. ranged from 2:05.52 – Robert Kiprono Cheruiyot winning the Boston Marathon — to more than 14 hours at the Honolulu Marathon.

Folks, if 14 hours doesn't make you feel better, nothing will. If you are the person who finished in 14 hours, we love you anyway.

In 2011, nearly 14 million people in the U.S. ran a road race. Fifty-four percent of those people were women, according to Ryan Lamppa, research statistician at Running USA. Lamppa predicts, "It's quite possible that women could make up 60 percent of finishers in the future. There is no doubt women will continue to drive the growth of the sport."

We've come a long way, baby, from the days when women were discouraged to run in fear their uterus would fall out. Or that they'd never bear children. Or my favorite: lose their *femininity*. Thank God some bright person somewhere worked this sh*t out before I got here.

I'm pretty excited women dominate recreational running. And I'm honored to be one of them. So today, I'm celebrating the stats, the sole sisters who have gone before us, and the simple joy of rockin' the road.

At I write this, I'm sitting in the doctor's office. I haven't eaten for 12+ hours. If you want to see angry, swing on by.

The Waiting Game

You knew I'd have to tell you.

Yesterday was all things fasting and ultrasounds. Two tests with pants on. The other, well, you can guess. I loved the technician. She's a 40-year-old mother of three – and she made things easy peasy. Thank God the tech wasn't a Bradley Cooper look-a-like. I'd have died.

When I get nervous, I run my mouth. And yesterday, during my tests, my mouth was in manic mode.

After Dr. Walker's in-depth review of the word "trans-vaginal" last week, I had no choice but to worry about what was to come. Three tests and $629 later, now I know.

I chatted the poor tech's head off the entire hour I was with her. Kids. Work. Educational history. Marathon training.

During my one-person run of mouth sh*t show, I asked if I could view the ultrasound screen while she worked. She obliged. (It pays to be nice to peeps, especially when you're half-neked.)

I got an up-close and very personal view of my gallbladder, kidneys, aorta, ovaries, spine, ribs, liver – the works.

There's something very weird about watching blood flow through your aorta. I was reminded of why I chose not to pursue a career in medicine. For starters, I'd be lousy at it. And second, my mouth would be permanently stuck on overdrive.

I asked why she wasn't rolling that lubed up piece of plastic over my intestines. She said, "There isn't usually much to see in that area." She's right. It's a dark black mass of all things air and blah. So not cool, but so the truth.

I then turned my charm-o-meter on high and asked if she detected anything I should be concerned about. She raised her brow, looked me dead in the eye and said, "I'm not allowed to diagnose."

Sh*t.

Have you noticed how many people have "raised their brow" at me in the last three months? Nearly everyone. Do you think it's me or have I unknowingly surrounded myself with only brow-raisers?

Not yet deterred, I inquired, "Would you know if something is wrong with me, even if you aren't allowed to say?" "Yes," she answers simply. Double sh*ts.

So, for now, we play the waiting game. And the waiting game in my world equates to further attempts at self-diagnosis.

As I think my side cramp may be linked to dehydration, I spent hours last night researching ideal hydration levels for endurance runners. (Okay, endurance/recreational runners.) It's crazy what you can find on Google. No matter which side of an issue you're on, you'll find data that supports your view.

Here's what I found:

The American College of Sports Medicine (ACSM) updated their guidelines in 2007. They no longer recommend specific volumes of fluid per hour (or guzzling). Their new recommendation? Drink when you're thirsty.

Cripes almighty! I am now an expert on water, hydration, dehydration, what color your pee should be, how often you should pee, what happens if you don't drink enough (and don't pee!) and if you drink too much and almost kill yourself with fluid.

Somewhere in the world there are people training for their first marathon who throw on their shorts, lace up their treads and hit the road. They likely pay no freakin' mind to the very sh*t that consumes me. But that's not how I roll. So I'll continue my quest for knowledge, health and all things marathon. And you can bet your a** you're coming with me.

All the way to the big, fat finish line.

*Hubs and I have a dart board in the basement. He bribes me to play by agreeing to blast 80s music while he hands me my a** on every game. Last night, I jammed to I LIKE IT by Dino. He's like, "Hey Brook, this should be your personal theme song." (That's the way it has to be 'cause that's the way I like it.)*

P*ssed Off Chi

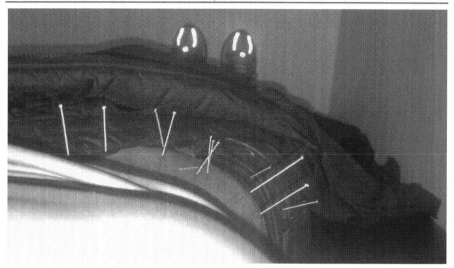

I decided it was time to expand my self-care protocol.

So yesterday, I added acupuncture to the mix.

When it was time for my session, the good doc told me to lay face up on the table. I was then ordered to do sit ups, backups, leg ups and every other kind of "up" known to man.

Of course, after this round of unanticipated calisthenics, I broke a sweat. Not a day goes by anymore where I don't freakin' sweat. For the love of all things holy, can't a girl catch a break?

Once the doctor ferreted out my pain, he revealed his magic box of needles.

As best I can tell, I was stuck 14 times. The pesky needle planted near my right hipbone woke and somewhat irritated my sleeping Chi. It didn't hurt, per say, but my energy force was definitely on high alert.

When all 12 needles were stationed in my abdomen, the doctor moved on to my legs.

I have struggled with shin splits and tight calves for months. When anyone gets near my legs, needles or not, I worry. He placed one needle below each knee, close to the top of my shins. Now my Chi is p*ssed off.

Good freakin' night! I must have the most stagnant Chi on the planet. For a moment I wondered if I was having a heart attack. I went so far as to ask, out loud, if that was possible.

For the next 15 minutes, I lay there and thought, "WTF have I done?" Maybe I'd have been better off leaving my "life force" alone.

All joking aside, acupuncture doesn't hurt. But you can feel something shift — whatever "something" is for you. It just gets a bad rap because peeps flip about needles.

I survived my 15-minute session. Afterward, I had a few life-sustaining errands to run. Dry cleaner, the grocery store and an impromptu stop at liquor world.

*Honestly, I'm tired of being poked and prodded. I'm over having appointments dictate my daily schedule. I'm feeling ready to get this f*ing show on the road already.*

At the grocery store, I caved and threw a small bag of Cheetos in my cart. I ate half the bag in the time it took me to drive home. I stopped at the neighborhood mailbox and threw the rest in the trash. Now those crunchy-fake-cheese-loaded-fattening-terrible treats can no longer tempt me. Until I buy the next bag, of course.

I'm wondering if training for a marathon is more about mental stamina than physical ability.

Some days it sure feels like it.

I read a quote the other day that has never been truer for me than it is right now:

"You've got what it takes, but it will take everything you've got."

Today I'm celebrating Chi, Cheetos and the final, final countdown.

A few weeks ago I shared that the police were in my neighborhood to stave off mayhem. Yesterday, I learned it was because a neighbor had tripped his house alarm. The end of the story isn't nearly as sexy as the beginning.

Everything Is Genius

Last night, I attended a hen party of epic proportions.

Okay, it was a Wednesday night, which means we all had our party muzzles on. That said, I spent a few hours catching up with some women I hold in very high-esteem.

I was in a hella good mood yesterday. First off, I had an amazing call with one of my clients. While chatting, she shared she's been reading all things Wayne Dyer and that his directive is helping shift her mind-set.

One of the key messages in his new book *Wishes Fulfilled: Mastering the Art of Manifesting* is:

"What if everything you've done (to this point in your life) is genius?"

I took this to mean: What if every single step, every single f* up, every single mistake, every single decision, every guy you married, every guy you didn't, your kids, your health, your money, your career — what if every last bit of everything you've done is absolute freakin' genius?

When I look at my life through that lens, I feel free.

If you're anything like me, you berate yourself constantly for the decisions you make. I should have run further. I can't believe I ate an entire sleeve of Girl Scout Cookies. I should have trained for a marathon in the summer. I should not have spent $312 on that fabulous new outfit. I can't believe I spent $629 on ultrasounds.

Everything I've done is genius.

I finally heard from the doctor yesterday. My ultrasounds came back clean. I'm enviously healthy for 36 years old.

For $629, he should have called me princess and organized a freakin' parade in my honor. He could have said I have the innards of an 18-year-old. What the hell has happened to customer service? Can't you deliver good news to your peeps and throw in a little extra awesomesauce?

I won't lie. I'm damn thankful I'm in tip-top shape. But, this means I still have to uncover what's causing the side cramp. That said, after hearing the results, I chastised myself.

"OMG. I just spent $629 dollars on tests only to learn I'm healthy."

Everything I've done is genius.

I spent time yesterday reading through a few old blog entries. You and me? We've been through a lot together in the last few months:

Extraterrestrials. Binge Eating. Melt-Downs. Breakthroughs. Monster Miles. Pee Machines. Sole Sisters. Skinny Jeans. Neked Pictures. Sh*t Weather. Organizing Hookers. Side Cramps. Gear. Gifts. Bad Attitudes. Rest Days. Sports Bras. Broken Bones. Heartburn. Trash. Money. Travel. Laughs. Tears. Trials. Triumphs.

Looking back, I can see I've done a lot of sh*t right chasing this dream. I also acknowledge I've made too many mistakes to count. But thanks to Wayne Dyer, now I know.

Everything I've done is genius.

This morning I applied some menthol sports cream to my ribs. Don't do that. It feels freakin' terrible. Everything I've done is genius...

White Hot Mess

This week has been one of my most social on record.

This means I'm not getting as much down time as I'd like. It seems the closer I get to race day the busier I become. Sh*t. Last night was dinner with Uncle Dan at the Chart House. Fantabulous. We caught up on family happenings, recent travels and summer plans.

Turns out Uncle Dan just bought a new piece of Caterpillar equipment. He offered to hook me up with his local sales rep to see if I could get a few more stocking caps.

The badge on mine is starting to peel, but what the hell. It has been washed more than 100 times and has been worn for well over 1,000 miles. I'm probably due.

At dinner, I splurged on red meat, mashed potatoes, and the biggest piece of ice cream cake I've ever encountered. Needless to say, my head hit the pillow at 8:45 p.m., and I was out cold — likely because of a self-induced sugar high.

This morning, Midas and I were up at 5:15 a.m. I stumbled to the closet and flipped on the light. The florescent overhead light has been flickering disco-like madness all week, which makes getting dressed that early even more of a challenge.

Fully clothed, I head to the kitchen and clip on my Shuffle. That's when I discern one ear bud is completely dead. But hey, my headphones have well over 1,000 miles on them, too. And who freakin' knows what those buds have been through tucked inside my ears for the last two years. Hooboy.

Note: I'd rather find this out today instead of tomorrow during my 22-mile throw down. I'll buy a new pair this afternoon, along with a spare to carry on race day.

I quickly reclaim an old pair from my bottomless junk drawer. The plastic on the ear pieces is so fossilized that they barely fit in my ears. They'll have to do.

Midas and I head to the garage, clip on our headlamps and away we go.

About a mile in, one of my all-time favorite songs, Iko Iko, begins to play.

And I start to cry.

I listened to Iko Iko five times in a row on my first ever 20-mile run a few weeks ago. I was four miles from the finish line and this song literally carried me two full miles. No joke.

It took me 10 minutes to pull myself together.

I am a white hot mess. (At least I know.)

It's crazy to think tomorrow is my last monster run before the marathon. The last few weeks will be tapering. Part of me is over-the-moon that the race is three weeks from Sunday. A small part of me is heartbroken that my first marathon journey is almost complete.

I made a very important decision this morning.

Whatever happens, whatever I happen to feel during this final countdown is okay. If I cry my head off every stinkin' day, so be it. If I laugh my a** off at the crazy sh*t guaranteed to unfold, I'm good with that too. I'm letting go of any and all judgments I have about what these last 22 days "should" look like and I'm going with it. I'm all in, baby.

So today, I'll spend a few hours preparing for tomorrow.

I'll swing by the chiro's office to have my back cracked. I'll snag two new pairs of ear buds from the Walgreens, and I have a 60-minute jam session scheduled with my psychic.

In this moment, I'm celebrating last hurrahs, lessons learned and leaning in.

A F*ing Haul

There ain't nothing easy about laying down 22 miles.

No matter how good you feel or how you splice and dice it, 22 miles is a f*ing haul. A lot of marathon trainees don't push past 20 miles in their training runs; I'm glad I did.

Today was the first time in *weeks* I wasn't scared to chase a big number. Last week's long run did wonders for my confidence.

Before now, I've completely psyched myself out about heartburn. Puking. Appendicitis-like cramps. Hydration. Dehydration. Bathroom business. Hunger. Gear. Miles. Every last thing I could dig up to worry about.

The cool part is all of my fears, all of my trials, and every last mile led me to this moment.

And today, I put 22 f*ing miles to bed.

Was it easy? Oh, hell no. Did I wonder a few times if I would actually get this done? Absolutely. Are my legs and dawgs crying? Hell, yes.

Here's how it went down:

As always, D.R., Andi and I rendezvoused before the sun came up. We said our heys, gave hugs, handed off gear and away we went. The temperature when we hit the trail was 47 degrees. By the time we finished, it was 70 freakin' degrees.

It was a solid, clean run until mile nine. I've never actually run more than nine miles out, so mentally it put me a little sideways. We kept running. And running. And running. (11 miles is the turnaround point.)

The temperature was on the fast track to hot-as-sh*t.

I am known for my Cat Hat. Hell, it's almost made me famous. I'm also known for my insane amount of layering. Since January, I have trained in near sub-freezing temperatures week after week after week. So yeah, I tend to favor warm's side of the fence. That said, my stinkin' layers almost killed me this morning.

As we turned to start our journey back, I realize we're still 2.5 miles from D.R, which meant I had no other choice but to keep my gear on until we reached her. (Okay, I probably could have stuffed all that sh*t in my pants, but I'm not that girl. Yet. On race day, I might be.)

Somewhere between mile 11 and 13, an a** hole on a bike nearly takes me out from behind. He's lucky I only had my legs available to me, or I would have chased him. He seriously came within a half inch of my arm. WTF?

If you're a cyclist, I love you. But don't DO THAT. It's freakin' rude.

Like a bright, shining beacon of hope, I finally see D.R. She's waiting patiently for us with water, snacks and alternate gear. I couldn't get my clothes off fast enough.

About that time, 179 bird watchers enter the scene. I had to make a choice.

- Either I could keep my long sleeve shirt on for another two miles,

- Or, I could strip down to my sports bra, show the world my duct-tape-ear-bud-brilliance and pull on a short-sleeved shirt.

I chose to bare skin. No one said this would be a modest or dainty endeavor. Off we went.

As we rounded the corner on 17 miles, I thought to myself, "Oh f*. We still have five miles to go."

Two miles later, I told Andi I needed a kick in the a** and put my ear buds in thinking tunes would carry me the distance. I rocked out to Train's Save Me San Francisco, which you already know is my marathon training mantra. It helped, but only a little.

Something happened (mentally) just after the 20-mile marker.

At 20 miles, it dawned on me that if today were race day, I'd still have 6.2 miles to go. For the love of all things holy, that's almost another half of a half marathon. Not only that, but my body was ready to quit. It was like, "Yeah, um, so glad we did this today. I did my part. I'm f*ing out of here."

That's when my mind grabbed the reigns.

With my brain firmly in the driver's seat, it used coercion and shame to propel my body forward.

"You're not weak! Sorry, we didn't come here to quit. We're going to lay this b*tch down with or without you, and we'd rather do it with you. Buck up. Keep trucking. The only way out is through."

And by God, we went through.

There isn't a song on the planet that could have saved me today. In fact, I tore my ear buds out after only a mile because the noise was an irritant. My mind was on a mission, and my entire being was forced to hunker down, dig deep and perform at a level never before imagined. It worked.

About a half-block from the finish, I start to walk. Andi looks at me and asks, "WTF are you doing? We're not there yet." So I ran all the way across the finish line.

To summarize, here are my lessons:

- I'd better have my gear down to a science on race day. I will start my race cold if need be. Andi suggested wearing a long sleeve t-shirt you don't mind losing, so you can peel it off and throw it away. The same goes for gloves. Buy a $1 pair of jersey work gloves and ditch 'em when it's time.

- Many-a-peep have mentioned running a marathon is a mental game. Now I know it's true. I don't care how many miles you've run during training or how long you train. Your mind and your heart will carry you across the finish line.

- I'm damn thankful I ran over 20 miles during marathon training. I would have never known how strong my mind is, or how easily it can command my body if need be.

Post-run, we walked over to the gas station to snag a few Gatorades. That's when Andi hands me a beautifully wrapped package. She says, "I have a gift for you; it's part homemade."

Inside, I find a Dr. Seuss *Cat In The Hat* book.

Only the words "in" and "the" have been whited out, which means I now have my very own "Cat Hat" book by Andi.

Here's how it ends:

"Have no fear of this run," said the Cat Hat. "I always take care of my awesome Brook Kreder. And you, my friend, are a marathon race raider."

Now I know. My mind, my heart, AND my Cat Hat will carry me home.

I'm registered to run a 5k tomorrow. Either I'm brilliant or bat sh*t. For now, I'm keeping with custom. I'm off to guzzle a margarita. Cheers!

Coming Full Circle

Day 99

I squeezed in a lot of livin' today.

I wasn't sure how I'd feel after yesterday's 22-mile throw down. Truth be told, last night my dawgs, legs and hip bones weren't just cryin', they were screaming. I could only hope a good night's sleep would usher in forgiveness from my lower extremities.

When Midas nudged me at 5 a.m., I laid silent for a few minutes. I thought to myself, "Oh f*. It can't possibly be time to get up. Is it Tuesday? If it's not, for the love of all things holy, leave me be." Midas isn't easily deterred.

So, I ever so slowly began to wiggle my toes. I rotated my ankles. Brought my knees up to my chest. Rolled my entire body to the right, then left. I gently lifted my arms to make sure they, too, were still attached. I was back in business.

Encouraged by my horizontal full-body assessment, I felt ready to further test my legs. Midas and I headed out for a two-mile leisurely stroll through the neighborhood. It was still dark, so I gave myself full permission to rock the PJs.

Hey, after yesterday's run, today felt like an anything goes kind of day. Just be thankful we're not neighbors.

Upon our return, I guzzled some much-needed coffee, chowed on a few pieces of cinnamon toast and showered up.

It was time to face the Cherry Creek Sneak.

The Cherry Creek Sneak holds a great deal of significance for me. Two years ago today, the Sneak was my first ever 5k. I trained for 4 freakin' months for that race, and I finished in 33 minutes. One year ago today, the Sneak was my first 5-miler. My goal was to run that entire race and I did, albeit run is a strong word.

I knew going back for the third time would feel like coming full circle.

So I layered up because God Almighty I didn't learn my lesson *yesterday*, and I drove down to battle 10,000 other runners for the same parking space.

Here's where this gets cool: About a month ago, I was chatting with my good friend Paula over breakfast. Of course, the only thing I can run my mouth about is all things marathon. (Big surprise.) She told me she had been running off and on for years and that she'd like to get back in the game.

I challenge her to run the Cherry Creek Sneak 5k with me. (Hey, it's put up or shut up around here. Again, be thankful we aren't neighbors.) She boldly says, "I'm in."

So this morning, I hook up with Paula about 30 minutes before the race. We hug, plaster our bibs to the front of our layers and make our way toward the starting line.

Five minutes before the gun goes off, I start to look around. I notice a Denver Police Bomb Squad Truck. And I think to myself, "Well THAT f*ing sucks."

I believe we've entered a new road race frontier. Gone are the days where race organizers could get away with hiring non-gun carrying security officers to keep order. Now it's dogs, guns and bomb squads.

Three minutes before the gun goes off, they release the visually impaired runners from the starting line.

And I think, "How awesome! For me, running with 20/20 vision is heroic.

Imagine running a race where someone else has to guide you. In that moment, I wished them a safe journey, and offered up a quick prayer of thanks that I can see.

Two minutes before the race starts, the announcer asks the crowd for a moment of silence to honor those affected by the bombings in Boston.

And I got tears in my eyes.

I thought about the runners, who just like me, showed up to run a race. Nothing more, nothing less. They likely felt the same emotions I was feeling that very minute — hopeful, excited, inspired, thankful. Each of the Boston Marathoners worked their a**es off just to get to the start line, let alone finish. In that moment, I sent prayers of safety, healing and health to all those affected, and to the entire city of Boston.

As I brought my focus back to the starting line, a single shot rang out. And we were off. I looked over at Paula and said, "Girl, this is your race. I'm hanging with you the entire way. If you want to run, we'll run. If you need to walk, we'll do that too."

And that's exactly what we did. We ran a little and walked a little. We chatted like school girls. Every time we had clear sight of another mile marker, we ran until we passed it. The last 3/10ths of a mile, I looked over at her and asked, "Girl, what do you think? Do you want to run to the finish line?"

"Absofreakinlutely," she smiled.

So we did. Paula found her stride and we rocked the road all the way to the end. About 20 paces from the finish, I teared up. (Again! I know!) She grabbed my hand and lifted both of our arms up in victory as we crossed the finish line.

In that moment, I was so freakin' proud of her. I was proud of her tenacity, her commitment, her refusal to quit, her ability to dig deep when it counted and to bring that 5k home.

I'm also proud of myself.

I realized just how far I've come as a person and as a runner. I've spent the last four months looking forward — chasing my big marathon dream. But today, for a brief moment, I got to look back at who I used to be and at how much running has changed me.

I'm so much stronger in every way a person can be. I am humbled and grateful.

Here are my lessons:

- Pay it forward. If you're a runner, and there is a non-runner in your circle of influence, challenge them. Be a mentor. Help them see what they maybe can't yet see for themselves. Witnessing someone else's journey to the finish line is magic.

- Honor how far you've come. We live in a forward facing world, which means we're in this constant space of next! next! next! The kindest thing you can do for yourself is acknowledge how far you've come.

Today, I'm celebrating friends, paying it forward and coming full circle.

Digging For Worry

I beat the hell out of myself on Saturday.

You spend your junior high years worrying someone else will beat you up. You get your first job post-college and wonder if your boss will take his failings out on you. Then you train for your first marathon and realize the only person's a** you're kicking is your own.

As race day looms, my curiosity about all things marathon is at an all-time high. (Think injuries, food, gear, race day, etc.)

Here are a few things I've been chewing on:

- If something goes terribly wrong and I have to bail on the marathon, how do you actually quit a race? Do you just walk off the course and make your way back to your car? What if you bail at mile 23? Do you walk 23 miles back to where you parked? (I obviously would call someone. Or I'd park my a** at the local tavern until someone fetched me.)

- A few weeks ago, when I shared that some runners wear Depends on race day, I thought it was hilarious. After that information hit the internet, I received a handful of emails from runners who told me they've bagged a race because of bathroom business. (So it's a real life concern.)

- What will I do if I'm injured in the weeks leading up to the race? (My left foot and knee have really taken a beating on the monster runs.) I can assure you, I would find some brave soul willing to prescribe or inject to mask my ails. I'm not proud. I'm honest.

My worries got me curious about what else I *should* be worried about.

You know, all the sh*t I'm not yet smart enough to ask on my own accord. I've come up through the school of hard knocks, and there are many things I haven't thought to ponder. I can't imagine I'm the only person on the planet who lets her mind run wild with absolutely-ridiculous-not-very-likely-one-in-a-freakin-gazillion-scenarios.

So this morning, I went digging for new sh*t to obsess over.

Here's what I found: Death. Endurance athletes who exercise for three hours or more have an increased chance of dying from cardiac arrest.

According to an article published by Peak Performance magazine, if you run marathons or participate in other forms of exercise that last for three hours or more, you have a 1 in 50,000 chance of suffering an acute heart attack or sudden cardiac death during or within 24 hours of your effort. (Note: Post-mortem analysis usually reveals that something was wrong with the runner's heart before the race.)

After reading this, I gladly hopped in to the recreational runner category. God almighty. Here you think you're doing your body and your bloody health a favor.

Iron Deficiencies. Runners Connect magazine shared that outside of training deficiencies, low iron levels in runners is of the most common reasons for poor results during workouts and races.

Recent research indicates almost 56 percent of joggers and competitive runners suffer from an iron deficiency that severely hampers performance. The article suggests most runners use iron supplements, unless their levels have previously tested high.

I spent 30 minutes in a "I'm iron deficient" forum for runners. They're chatting about hair loss, extreme fatigue and brittle fingernails. Good news is, if I am iron deficient, I'm somehow managing to keep my hair.

Body Weight. Body weight is the second most talked about topic among runners. (Injuries are first.)

Runners who attempt to lower their body fat percentages to dangerous levels run the risk of injury, illness, infertility, and at the very least, decreased performance.

Losing weight has been the furthest thing from my mind, as evidenced by my cinnamon roll, ice cream lovin', margarita and Mexican food blow outs. It's post-marathon calories that keep me up at night.

Injuries. According to the American Academy of Physical Medicine and Rehabilitation, nearly 70 percent of runners will become injured. While many of their injuries will appear minor, they can become more serious over time if not properly treated.

It takes between 30,000 and 50,000 steps to run a marathon. (Oh f*.)

Every time the foot hits the ground, a stress three to four times your body weight is absorbed by the ankles, knees, hips and lower back. (My "stress" factor maxes out at 516 pounds.) Fortunately, relatively few marathon runners have experienced injuries while running a marathon that caused them to seek medical attention.

Heat. An article published on Marathon.com outlines — of all the adversities runners and marathoners face, heat is the number one offender. This is because it can bring on two conditions that can negatively affect your performance: overheating and dehydration.

There are hundreds of articles covering races where runners either died or were adversely affected by heat. I got a small sampling of how mean-spirited rising temperatures can be on Saturday. God as my witness, I'll tear off every last piece of clothing and cross the finish line in compression socks and treads if that's what it takes.

T-Minus 24 Hours. Author Vincent Healy writes, "Eat well the night before, but be careful not to eat too much. Get a good night's sleep. It is more crucial to sleep well two nights before the marathon, and sleep only adequately the night before."

Nearly every marathoner I've talked to said they were tormented by their last supper and by sleeping enough the night before. The good news is I've been tweaking my pre-run meal for months and I sleep like I'm dying.

After all this research, am I seriously worried about any of these ailments? No. Do I think it's good to know? Absofreakinlutely.

But Pat Schroeder said it best, "You can't wring your hands and roll up your sleeves at the same time."

And I'm a roll up my sleeves kind of gal myself.

My magical P.O. Box netted a kick a** postcard from my good friend Jack. It said, "We Live for This Sh*t." He's so freakin' right.

Almost To Vegas

If I had been running in a straight line, I'd be creeping up on Las Vegas.

Starting a movement journal has been one of the best things I've done to date. If there is ever a time I don't feel I've done enough, all I have to do is look at my mile log to see how far I've come.

When researching marathon-training programs, I found varying opinions and approaches. Some experts say beginning marathoners should log at least 35 miles a week. (Check!) More experienced runners can likely run a sub-three hour race by logging 40-55 miles per week.

Listen. If you're logging anywhere near 55 miles per week, I'm freakin' cheering for you. But I also wonder how the hell you're getting anything else done. A 55-mile week would be five 11- mile runs per week. Holy Cripes.

Since I began training, I've logged 555.69 miles running and 717.74 miles total. As of today, I'd be approximately 53 miles from Las Vegas. It's 608 miles between Denver and Sin City. Oh, the things I would do if I were actually almost there. It would be both inspiring and ugly.

Here's how April shook out:

April	Total-To-Date
Ran: 159.5 miles	Total Running: 555.69 miles
Walked: 10.84 miles*	Total Walking: 93.55 miles
Hiked: 8 miles	Total Hiking: 20 miles
Biked: ZERO	Total Biking: 48.5 miles
Midas Total: 86.34 R/W/H	Midas T-T-D: 333.08 miles

Note: The biggest change in the last 30 days is I ditched the 2-a-day program. The extra afternoon walks had to go; they were stressing my shins past the point of no return.

Rolling into March, I moaned about how my training schedule that month terrified me. My long runs were 18, 13, 18, 10 and 14. Had I known then what I know now, April's long runs would have had me sobbing in the fetal position. (20, 18, 20, 22.)

April ushered in both chaos and enlightenment.

I ran through telling trash; My first 20-mile throw down; 16 bags of pretzels courtesy of Delta Airlines; moss agate rocks; Depends undergarments; pity parties; a Jewish wedding; the bombings in Boston; a negative pregnancy test; ultrasounds; 14 hours in Honolulu; p*ssed off Chi; Dr. Seuss; my first ever 22 mile run; and finally coming full circle.

You have no idea when you start what your body can actually do with some training and coercion. You also have no freakin' clue what the road has in store. So every day, the only thing you can do is show up with a good attitude, a strong will and trust what you're doing is enough.

Today, I'm celebrating the fact that if sh*t gets messy 'round here, I can run to Vegas.

I'm off to have my body fat measured today. After last night's blow out on chocolate chips it's anybody's guess where I'll land.

Sheer F*ing Madness

Day 102

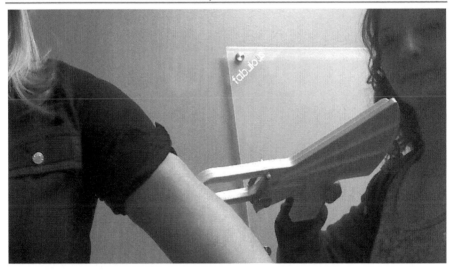

Yesterday, I had my body fat measured.

Anyone who has ever had a skin fold caliper latched to any part of their body knows nothing that piece of plastic does is flattering.

I was tempted to keep my eyes and ears shut while Shari took measurements. But I couldn't help but be curious about the results. (I am a Type A, borderline anal personality if you haven't heard.)

The first time I ever had my body fat measured was 3 years ago. I was 33 years old. I was walking Midas a few miles a day, 300 times a year. We were hiking the hills by our house a few times a month. My a** wasn't as tight as I'd have liked, but I figured I could blame it on age. I was as fit as I cared to be. (Or so I thought.)

I remember waking up one day in April, showering, and pulling on my shorts. I looked down and noticed the skin on the front of my legs was starting to sag.

WTF?

I was mortified.

Seriously, at 33, I was nowhere near okay with my skin sagging. I am a retired Jazzercise instructor. (Embarrassing, but true.) I thought I was doing my part by hoofing it around the neighborhood almost daily. Obviously, my efforts were enough to keep me trim, but not tone. It was time to regain control of the situation. Like pronto.

Enter my personal trainer Shari. I called her in a panic. "Can you get me in today?" I pleaded. I didn't get in that day, but I did get in that week.

The first time I entered her studio, I was scared. She has a huge room full of very expensive contraptions that look like they could chew you up, spit you out and leave you beggin' for your ever-lovin' life. It was the big leagues compared to my eight-pound hand weights hidden behind the treadmill in my basement.

Before we talked strategy, she weighed me and measured my body fat. That was my first encounter with the mean-spirited skin-fold caliper.

I'm not sure what I weighed at the time, but my body fat rang in at 18 percent.

Shari and I went to work on crafting a simple, 10 minutes a day, strength-training program that would tighten me up. We settled on 10 minutes because that was all I was willing to commit. I also told her I wasn't prepared to give up bread or vodka. (Some things never change.)

After 30 days, I gained weight. But I lost 3 percent body fat. Yes, in 10 minutes a day, with a piece of bread in one hand and a vodka tonic in the other. I won't bore you with the rest of the story, but 18 months later, I went back to Shari to be re-measured. It was the same year I started running.

My body fat had dropped 7 percent.

Fast forward to yesterday. I've run 559.69 miles since I started training. But I've also probably consumed close to 4 billion calories. I thought for sure my body fat would be lower than it was 18 months ago.

It was the exact same.

My mind went bat sh*t. What the f*! How in the world can my percentage be the exact same? Doesn't my body remember all of those three hour runs over the last two months? What the hell is going on?!?!? Seriously?

Shari and I spent some time discussing body fat in general.

Essential fat in women is 8 to 10 percent. Anything lower ventures into unhealthy territory and your body can start leeching calcium from your bones. You also need body fat to absorb vitamins, keep body heat, and have energy and focus.

I'm sharing this today for two reasons:

- Doing 10 minutes a day of strength training can make a huge difference in your overall health. It can also benefit your marathon training, tremendously. It's hard to believe such little effort can net big results, but over time, it can.

- When you start training for anything -- a 5k, a triathlon, Tough Mudder, whatever – measure everything. (I know I've said this one hundred times.) Take pictures. Start a journal. You may not see outrageous gains in every area, but when you do, it's reason enough to keep truckin'.

Today I'm celebrating measurements, mean-spirited skin fold calipers and the sheer f*ing madness of training for a marathon.

If you're comparing your numbers to mine, please don't. Everyone's journey is personal. I noticed Shari's biceps yesterday and almost starting crying; they're freakin' fabulous. But I've learned. "Thou shall not covet thy trainer's biceps."

Cute As Sh*t

A few days ago, I got an email that lit a fire under my a**.

Andi sent me a picture of the shirt she plans to wear on race day. Her note said, "Hot neon pink. Racer back. Thinnest mesh possible. Won't miss this!"

As I know she's Miss Speedy Gonzalez, I will probably see her shirt at the start line and when she's waiting for me at the finish.

It lit a fire because I'm rounding the corner on burning down my first marathon and I have no f*ing idea what I'm going to wear.

Sans one outing, I've worn pants on every single long run for 18 weeks. Ten of those weeks, I wore ancient long underwear under those pants, which means I haven't yet had the opportunity to put potential race-day gear through the chafe test.

I normally don't care what I look like when I run. I'm usually so focused on surviving the miles that I couldn't give a damn how I represent. That said, I have a sneaking suspicion I'll take more photos on race day than I did on my wedding day.

Since I said, "Yes!" to training for my first marathon, I've had this vision I'd cross the finish line in a skirt. And look cute as sh*t doing it.

I have since let go of cute as sh*t. After all, I can't really control all of THAT after 26.2 miles. But I haven't let go of the skirt.

A few days ago I ran over to my local running store to see if they had any dresses. Nope. So I was forced to hop online and poke around. Slim pickings, baby.

But I finally found one. I like the color and it happened to be a staff favorite. So I ordered two different sizes hoping one fits. And forever the Diva, I ordered the compression socks and sun sleeves to match.

Hey, you only run your first marathon once, right? I told Hubs I was

kicking around a dress and he's like, "WTH? You never wear a dress."
And he's right. I don't. "So, why in the world would you wear one to run
a freakin' marathon?" My only comeback was, "Because I want to."

'Nuff said.

Here's the deal: Wearing new gear on race day is a Cardinal Sin. And
with only two long runs left, I know my window to "chafe test" is
closing.

This prompted me to pay the $17 rake-you-over-the-coals expedited
shipping fee so I could have this polyester/spandex/leopard print
contraption in my hands before Saturday's hoopla. Where is heck
Amazon Prime when you need it?

Here's where this gets problematic: This morning it was 20 degrees in
Denver. (Weather.com said it "felt like" 5 degrees.) If it's 20 freakin'
degrees on Saturday there's no way on God's green earth I'll be testing
this dress. I don't care that I'm a hearty girl from Nebraska, that's far too
cold to run around with half neked legs.

Whatever I end up wearing, here's what I know for sure: "It is ever so
much easier to be good if your clothes are fashionable." – L.M.
Montgomery

Ain't that the freakin' truth.

Instead of being faithful about applying sunscreen, I've been chasing my
own a** with sun spot remover. I finally realized sunscreen would not
only be more effective, but cheaper, too. (I can be slow.) Sunscreen
containing Titanium Dioxide and Zinc Oxide comes highly recommended
by skin care professionals.

Finally, An Explanation

Yesterday's list of activities included a 90-minute massage.

I spent 15 minutes before I left the house looking for scientific and/or medical reasons a massage was necessary. Then I threw in the towel and said f* it. The simple fact that I wanted one was reason enough.

The therapist and I chatted the full 90 minutes. We both love The Voice. We both cry during movies, sad or not. We love dogs and good girlfriends and we both hate to shop. (She's so my peep.)

Anyhoo, when the conversation ventured around to the marathon, I told her I had been an emotional wreck for the last few months. I confessed, "I cry all the freakin' time! I cry over Neil Diamond songs. I cry when I visualize crossing the finish line. I cry over the awesomeness of this entire experience."

Okay, sometimes I just get tears in my eyes but to me, it's the same.

She came back with, "You cry all the time because you're moving a ton of energy in your body."

Finally. An explanation.

She further interpreted, "Movement of any kind, and especially sweat, pushes energy in, around and out of your body. It's a good thing."

Here's what's crazy: She was the *fourth* person this week to "school" me about energy.

Yes, I'm a God-fearing girl. That said, I believe metaphysical principles and theories have a place. I'm the first to admit I enjoy listening to (and learning from!) people much smarter than I about all things Universe. I'm glad there are peeps in the world willing to share their brilliance because, truth be told, none of this is anywhere near my Zone of Genius.

With her expertise established, I decided to dig deeper. Hell, I'm neked on her table anyway, which means she's already seen the best and worst of me. What do I have to lose?

"I feel like my physical sh*t is suffocating me," I whisper. "Intuitively, now seems like the right time for an epic-purge-of-all-things-tangible." Think books. Old files. My entire office. My closet. My kitchen. Junk drawers. Everything. The way I feel right now goes far, far, far beyond spring-cleaning.

She asserted, "That's normal, too."

Apparently, as you change on the inside, i.e., limiting beliefs, feelings, thoughts, etc., you can't help but crave change in your physical environment, as well.

She summed up our conversation with, "Who you are *now* isn't who you used to be. As you shed things energetically, of course you'll feel compelled to purge physical items. Those items no longer reflect or support who you have become."

I have seriously run around for the last 90 days questioning my sanity. I've been a bit out-of-sorts and mildly embarrassed that my tear ducts were set on overdrive. Now I know, I've just been metamorphosing into a better, stronger version of me. I can so live with that.

Today I'm celebrating massages, metaphysical principles and metamorphoses of epic proportions.

I shared this because many marathon-wanna-bes experience all kinds of shedding while training. You're not crazy. And I've got your back.

Nothing More, Nothing Less

My good friend Christine hoofed it five miles with me today.

The cool part is I haven't run alone in weeks. When I started this journey I had no idea how many sole sisters I had. Trust me, we're everywhere.

Last night, she texted that she was having Chicken Enchiladas for dinner. And I'm thinking, "Why the f* would she text me that?" She texts again, "Hope I don't have gas tomorrow! Ha ha." I quickly responded, "Sister, all joking aside, who cares. It's game on. Anything goes."

Listen. I'm the first to admit you can't always control what happens while you're on the trail. Sometimes you have to pee. Sometimes you have to toot. There's not a damn thing you can do about either except honor your body. If you ever run with me, I'll tell you right now, anything goes. Albeit if you sh*t your pants, I'm turning you over to D.R. and she can handle you.

Back to this morning -- Christine and I met up and she handed me a ginormous box of treats.

All of my friends are Goddesses in the kitchen. Why didn't I get this skill? Every long run these past few weeks has been nothing less than a social throw down. Andi regularly brings truffles. Today, Christine brought her awesomeness to share. I could easily inhale more calories than I burn if I put my mind to it.

With the treats safely packed in my cooler, we say hi to D.R., catch up on what's new and good, do the hand off, and away we go.

Christine was worried she'd slow me down. Not so. We kept a great pace the entire five miles --and don't kid yourself, we chatted our heads off. It's *amazing* what you can cover in 50 minutes.

The miles flew by. Before I realized it, it was already time to part ways. She was headed to her son's Lacrosse game. And me? I push on for 8.1 more miles.

For the first time in weeks, I found myself alone on the trail.

So I turned up the tunes and found my legs. It was go-time, baby. I breezed to the turnaround point. I spent damn near half an hour in awe of how good I felt. I remember my first 14-mile run a few months back and how scared I was. How freakin' *hard* it seemed.

As I roll up on D.R. at mile eight, she's shaking her head. She said, "Girl, do you remember how big of a deal it was for you to run all the way to Starbucks? (The seven-mile point.) How we'd both hold our breath hoping you'd make it? Today, this seems so easy for you. What a difference."

And she's right. It's wild to be on the backside of what I consider the big leagues. (18, 20 and 22 miles.) That's likely what made today's 13.1 throw down seem so dang much easier.

Today, I fell back in love with running.

Hey, if you get a charge out of laying the big boys down week after week, I salute you. But me? I have to earn those numbers. And it's freakin' hard. There were many a day when those monsters tried to kill me — and a few times, they almost did.

That's why this morning was so special. I ran for the simple joy of it. Nothing more, nothing less.

Here are my lessons:

- Invite other sole sisters to run with you. I guarantee your miles will go faster. And you just might push them a little farther than they'd go on their own.

- If you lose your love of the road, you're f*ed. For the past four weeks, I've beat the hell out of myself on the trail, and honestly, it wasn't that much fun. Are you a warrior when you lay down 22 miles? Absofreakinlutely. But fun seems like too strong of a word. Hold on to your love of running for dear life. It will bring you back if you happen to lose your way.

Today I'm celebrating treats, tunes and the love I have again for all things running.

This morning, I gave my new compression socks a go. Apparently, they make socks specifically for your left foot and your right foot. I didn't know.

The Secret Playbook

Today marks the official 14-day countdown to my marathon.

To celebrate, I am sharing my fool-proof formula, i.e., the blow-by-blow for how you, too, can train for your first marathon. Enjoy!

BK's Short, 14-Step Guide to Running a Marathon

Step 1: Decide.

After your spouse (who is a marathoner) has goaded you for months, finally say, "Yes! Fine! Cool! OK! I will run a marathon." Get excited. Connect with your "I'm all-kinds-of-in-on-this" swagger. Completely ignore the small voice in your head screeching, "WTF! Absolutely not! There's no way we're doing this!" Celebrate by telling everyone in your inner circle — "I'm going to be a marathoner." Appreciate how good your body feels because it won't feel this good again for a freakin' *year*.

Step 2: Tell Your Peeps.

Check yourself into a dingy a** hotel room. Get a f*ing brilliant idea to start a blog because telling your inner circle peeps simply isn't enough. Get on Wordpress.com and recklessly click a bunch of buttons. Just $200 and a unique URL later, you've got a place to tell your story. Commit to blogging daily because there is no way a few days a week would be enough, right? Start a Facebook page and hope 100 people will "Like" what you're up to. After you've run 21 days in a row on a treadmill, realize training for a marathon in the winter might not be the smartest thing you've ever done.

Step 3: Craft Your Marathon Training Schedule.

Sit down with your Runners World Calendar, (a Christmas gift from your mother-in-law), and chart your course to 26.2. Recognize that for the next 20 weeks, your social life will be in the sh*tter. Start sweating as you write down the numbers 16, 18, 20, 22 — over and over again. Think to yourself, "Oh f*. What have I done?" For the first time ever, consider you might be in over your head. Share your training calendar on your blog as a warning to others.

Step 4: Documentation and Measurements.

Ask your spouse to take neked pictures of you under the only freakin' florescent light in your house. Don't think to move them to a safer place. Blind your brother when he's exposed to your husband's bare a** during an impromptu photo shoot. Beg for forgiveness. Send him an apology card. Measure your biceps, boobs, rib cage, waist and hips. Write down, in a secret-secret place, how much you think you weigh. Start a daily movement journal. After 100 days, realize you're almost to Vegas. Wish you were in Vegas. Near the end of training, weigh yourself. Have your body fat tested. Note neither has changed. Get sad. Get p*ssed. Be damn thankful your primary reason for running a marathon wasn't weight loss.

Step 5: Channel Martha Stewart.

As your miles increase, admit you've become addicted to Mexican food and cinnamon rolls. Buy a bottle of the generic heartburn pills your Mom recommended. Binge on Cheetos, pita chips and strawberry shortcake. Come home from a run and throw all that sh*t in the trash. Buy more Cheetos, pita chips and strawberry shortcake. Throw that sh*t in the trash, again. Get smart. Channel Martha Stewart. Make a year's worth of meals in one night and put them in the freezer. Get irritated because you were under some kind of false impression you could eat anything you wanted while training for a marathon.

Step 6: Gear up.

Wake up one day and notice every last piece of running gear you own is freakin' ratty. Convince yourself its okay to spend money on new clothes, after all, you're taking a sh*tload of pictures for your blog, right? And because you're training for a marathon, you have a grave responsibility to look cute as sh*t doing it. Hit up your local sporting goods store half a dozen times. Lay down good money to buy every last piece of name brand clothing you can find. After each item has been washed and tested, suffer a terrible case of buyer's remorse because some of your purchases were less than brilliant.

Step 7: Runner's Safety.

After three people call to share an assault incident that went down near your house, decide to take safety seriously. Get a Road ID bracelet. Start carrying mace. Pray to God you never spray yourself. Develop your own personal brand of ugly whoop a** via a self defense class. Hire a support person for your long runs. Celebrate that she has her concealed weapons permit. Also celebrate the fact you no longer have to carry your own water.

Step 8: Develop a Bathroom Strategy.

On your first outdoor long run, realize every public restroom along the trail is closed. Again, acknowledge training for a marathon in the winter might be a bad idea. Be thankful your support person is crafty enough to build you a custom pee machine. Learn from other people that some runners wear Depends on race day. Convince yourself it's a bold lie until a handful of your new Facebook peeps email to say it's true. Add "sh*tting of the pants" to your list of things to worry about.

Step 9: Learn to Run on the Run.

With travel looming, buy every last box of Clif Bars you can find. Stuff them in your suitcase. Pray the baggage handler's sniffer is broker. Pay the checked bag fee. Turn your gear over to people who eat small children for breakfast. Pray again that your sh*t shows up. Be nice to the flight attendants. Ditch your pride and beg for snacks. Offer up thanks when they stuff 16 bags of pretzels and a biscotti cookie in your purse. Hop into an unmarked, white taxi cab that reeks of stale cigarettes. Save your own a** by feigning love and interest of all things Star Castle. Offer up thanks (again!) when a complete stranger throws a $10 bill on your lap so you can regulate your blood sugar.

Step 10: Know When to Fold 'Em.

Several weeks in to your training schedule, bail on a 14-mile run because of a crippling side cramp. A few weeks later, bag an 18-mile run because your heartburn is so f*ing bad you nearly puke. Sit on the park bench and chew on how to gracefully tell 2,100 of your closest friends on Facebook that you can't stand how puke feels blasting through your nostrils. Wonder why you ever started a Facebook page. Wonder why you started a blog. Wonder why no one told you some long runs will be a sh*t storm. Refuse to quit. Come back for more. Hand yourself your own a** on an 18-mile run. Then a 20. Learn that pride is enough.

Step 11: When It Takes Over Your Life.

Somewhere around the 90-day mark, you realize training for a marathon has consumed you. Your non-runner friends stop calling you back. Your co-workers turn and high tail it when they see you. Your spouse thinks you're bat sh*t. Your dog is the only one who is all in on this because you're his ticket out of the yard. Date night includes a trip to the running store. You pinky swear you will *not* talk about the marathon. You fail miserably. You wonder what you used to think about. You wonder if you'll ever think about anything else again. You cry your head off. In gratitude. In fear. In total disbelief that you will very likely finish a marathon.

Step 12: Host a Few Pity Parties.

As you round the corner on month four, start feeling sorry for yourself. Your dawgs f*ing hate you. So do your hipbones. Your back is bloody from your mean spirited sports bra. You realize you can't walk up (or down!) the stairs in your house without wincing. Ice is your new BFF. You've perfected the John Wayne swagger. You have an ace bandage in every room of your house. You rub menthol sports cream on your rib cage. It burns holes in your skin. You lay down $700 on tests, only to learn that you're not pregnant. You dig deep. Get over yourself. Get on with training.

Step 13: Coming Full Circle.

As race day looms, you take a peek in the rear view mirror. You hardly recognize yourself. The skin on your face is beat to sh*t. It looks like leather. Your dawgs have tried to divorce you. Your knees are on the verge of quitting. So is your heart. Your back has permanent callouses from your sport bra. The tread on your race day shoes is worn down to nubbies. By some miracle, you've managed to run through most of your baggage, bullsh*t, blowouts and breakdowns. You wake up and realize you're two weeks away from burning down your first marathon.

Step 14: Celebrate T-Minus 14.

You wake up and run your dog five miles. You realize it's Cinco De Mayo. You thank God, finally, a legitimate reason to drink a margarita. Maybe five. You decide it's time to share your top-secret playbook for *how* to train for a marathon. You write down 14 steps, one for each day left in the game. You wonder if you've included everything. You wonder if you've covered your a**. You wonder if someone somewhere will want to kiss you for giving it to them straight. You wonder if someone somewhere will want to punch you in the mouth. You realize it's anybody's guess. You head off to the Mexican restaurant, knowing you've done your best.

A Sole Strategy

I currently own six pairs of running shoes.

Four pair of ASICS. One pair of Brooks. And an older-than-dirt pair of Sketchers. It's anybody's guess how many miles, combined, these shoes have on them. Very likely a few thousand. Maybe more. Half of them have been stuffed in the back of my closet for the last year. They'll definitely make the great purge-of-all-things-tangible post-marathon.

I'm kind-of embarrassed to share that I started my modest running career in Sketchers. But it's true. It didn't take long to figure out those treads weren't doing me any favors.

So I put down some good money and invested in my first pair of ASICS. I ran/walked in those ASICS for almost a year. Then I hit up a local sporting goods store, (still not yet brave enough to walk into running specialty store), and laid down $184 on the sh*ttiest pair of ASICS ever made.

I loved those shoes. But I was a sucker. I thought expensive meant bad-a**.

So, so, stupid, and a lesson I've learned a hundred times training for a marathon.

They were one of the only pair ASICS ever made with gel placed on the *outside* of the shoe. (You think I would have known enough to know that's a damn bad plan.) Needless to say, not my smartest purchase.

The next pair I bought was also ASICS. They are the shoes I plan to wear on race day. The tread is worn down to the nubbies. They have holes on top. They are the only pair of treads I own that have *not* resulted in a long run sh*t storm.

Here's where this starts to come together: Two months into marathon training, I knew it was time to expand my footwear options.

Hey, every runner knows shoes last between 400 to 600 miles. Even newbies recognize it's freakin' R-A-R-E to start and end your marathon training in the same pair of shoes. And trust me, you know when you're due. Every last joint in your body is beggin' for mercy.

So I splurged and picked up a new pair of Brooks. I loved them, too. They came highly recommend by the experts at the specialty store, and God knows what they tell you at the specialty store is law, right?

I was wearing those treads when I called my first long run of the season. My appendicitis cramp morphed into a "I-think-we-can-kill-Brook-today-let's-give-it-a-whirl" monster. I blamed the cramp solely on those shoes. So they went in the "cute with jeans pile."

A month later, I tried again. Hubs and I swing through the running specialty store on date night. I buy the same exact pair of ASICS I currently own. (Only a little uglier.) Then I foolishly test them on my first 20-miler. Yeah. Um, a damn bad plan. I finished that run, but by the skin of my freakin' teeth.

I share this because in my humble opinion, developing a "sole strategy" is just as crucial as laying out your training schedule. Personally, I'd recommend having two or three pairs of treads you can rotate through on your long runs. That way none get too worn, and you have more than one option on your big day.

So I'm back to my older-than-Jesus-beat-to-sh*t-holes-on-top-dead-tread ASICS for race day. But that's okay because I know their "git-er-done" attitude will get me where I'm a going.

In 2010, U.S. running-shoe sales rose to $2.36 billion. I've more than done my part.

Learning The Lingo

Right now, I'm in what's called the taper period.

Let me tell you how I learned about the dreaded taper. I had just blogged about rest days, i.e., how hard it was, mentally, to take a day off from training. Someone on Facebook threw out, "You think rest days are hard sister, just wait until you have to taper!"

I quickly responded, "WTH is a taper? Is that post-marathon? Is that the period during the race when your organs start to shut down? Is it the terrible depression you face post-marathon?"

I was worried.

Luckily, my girlfriend stepped in and said it's the period before a marathon when you decrease your miles to physically and mentally prepare for race day.

FYI: So far, I've loved every stinking day of my taper. I'm damn thankful someone thought this might be a good idea. If I had to run 22+ miles for three f*ing weeks leading up to the race ... Well, let's just say sh*t 'round here would have been messy.

This morning, I was thinking about my taper. I also laughed at how much I've learned and how much I didn't know when I started. Long-time runners throw around all these wild a** terms, and assume, because I'm training for marathon, I know what they mean. I usually don't.

Left to my own devices, I have either Googled the term/word/acronym or I feigned brilliance and pretended to know what they were talking about.

Well, no more.

I finally took the bull by the horns and researched every last stinkin' term I think I should know as I prepare to be a marathoner.

Here's what I learned:

Top 25 Words and Terms Every Runner Should Know So They, Too, Can STOP Leaning On Google And START Living a Brilliant Runner's Life:

Bonk — Crashing in a race because you run out of fuel, i.e., hitting the wall. (I'm f*ing bonked, bonking and bonkers all the time. I wonder if it's all the same.)

Carbo load — A garbage truck full of pasta and French bread.

Chute – The area directly after the finish line. (I hope I actually see the freakin' chute.)

CR — Course Record. Also short for Crappy Race.

DNF, DNS, DFL, DNC – Did Not Finish, Did Not Start, Dead F*ing Last, Do Not Care.

DNR — Do Not Resuscitate. It means if I die, please, for the love of all things holy, leave me be.

Fartlek — Swedish for "speed play," or running irregular distances at varying speeds. It's not a synonym for gas. Sorry.

Flopper — A runner who has a habit of collapsing in dramatic fashion after they cross the finish line. It's still anybody's guess if I'll fit into this category. I may be a pre-finish line flopper. We'll see.

Grinder – A hill. (If your mind went immediately to the gutter, that's okay. Mine did, too.)

Drop The Hammer – What you've got left at the end to finish strong or pull away for the win. (Yeah. Right.)

Kick — A quick surge that carries you over the finish line. DNA — does not apply.

LSD — It's not what you think. Short for Long, Slow Distances. My interpretation: Let's Slow Down.

MP, GMP — Marathon Pace, Goal Marathon Pace. (Mine is SAS — Slow as Sh*t.)

MPD — Miles Per Day. (TM — far Too freakin' Many.)

Negative Splits — Running the last half of the race faster than the first. (Are you freakin' kidding me? Does this actually happen?)

NKA – No Known Allergies. (I have this on my Road ID. If you want to load me up with Valium or Morphine, go for it.)

NRF — Non-Running Friend. (The peeps who stop returning your call when you're training for a marathon. You know who they are.)

NRR — Not Running Related. (Nothing in my life fits in this category right now. So DNA.)

PR, PB, PV, PW — Personal Record, Personal Best, Personal Victory, Personal Worst. (My first marathon will fit under all of these — woot!)

Romp n' Chomp – Morning run with a meal after. (My new favorite term!)

Seeing Elvis – Running out of your comfort zone. Taxing your body to the point where you see Elvis, Jimi Hendrix, Jim Morrison and Janis Joplin. (Carry a notebook, you may have the chance to snag an autograph.)

Sit On – To lag behind someone, waiting to kick. (I'll be sitting on everyone race day — look for me. I'm the DFL chick in the cute as sh*t dress.)

Surge — A tactical move somewhere in the race when you move quickly by another runner. At least I'll know what to call it as other runners zip by me. Oh, a surge. Look, another one! And another! If I keep allowing this to happen I will be DFL. Better bring the hammer.

Turnover – How many steps you take during a minute of running. (I would have thought this was turning over in your freakin' grave after you died on race day.)

Zombie Zone — The spot you find during a race, just outside of your comfort zone. Warning: This is where you might just see Elvis.

So here's my plan: A carbo load followed by a killer bonk. A PR, PB, and a PV even if I'm DFL. I DNC. If I make it to the chute, I'll go pro-flopper. I will have a pen and paper handy for the Zombie Zone, where I plan to chat up Elvis. Finally, I'll drop the hammer and high tail it over to the post-race phase of romp n' chomp.

Already A Winner

These days, I'm sliding in sideways all over the place.

I don't like to feel rushed. In fact, I can't stand it. I'm the girl who leaves for the airport four hours early to make sure I make the gate on time. If I have somewhere to be, I prefer to be early -- even if it means checking email in the parking lot for 30 minutes. Hey, if you are one of those people who can go with the flow, I salute you. But, the truth is, I am a certified freaker.

I'm leaving for Wyoming in a few, which means that yesterday I had to get all kinds of strategic with my schedule. I was on the hunt for time to run, blog, sleep, eat, see peeps, snag a cocktail, see more peeps, snag another cocktail, get my freakin' hairs cut and have a few kick-a** client sessions.

I love to be busy, so this isn't a plea for pity.

But, when you choose to throw "train for a marathon" into the mix, sh*t can get messy.

I haven't washed my car in two months. (Hey, no judging.) I have yet to call the repair man to fix my oven. (I hate to cook so this is a bit of a blessing.) My favorite place to shop these days is Amazon because I'll have whatever it is in my hands within two freakin' days, and I don't have to leave my house. (Thank you, Jesus, for the person who thought to offer free shipping.)

Here's where I'm going: While I was out pounding pavement this morning, I thought to myself, "Good freakin' night. Sometimes just navigating life can be a heroic effort, let alone making time to run an a** load of miles, travel, work, etc."

My mind then moved to the women marathoners I interviewed when I began training. I thought about their stories, what they conquered to cross the finish line, and the wisdom they shared.

I asked each of them to describe the high of their experience, the low, what they did scared, and the one thing they wanted me to know about training for my first marathon.

Nearly all of them said: Enjoy the journey.

And I was like, what the hell does that mean? How do you "enjoy" 18 and 20-mile throw downs? How do you love bagging a run, blowing out on Cheetos and bawling your eyes out daily? At the time, I wasn't smart enough to ask them how to enjoy the process. I have a sneaking suspicion they wouldn't have handed over the "how-to" anyway because every single person's adventure to their first marathon is different.

This morning, it all came together.

When I was training for my first half marathon, my head was down the entire freakin' time. I took a hugely methodical (and boring!) approach, which didn't leave a lot of room for magic. After crossing the finish line on race day, they scanned my bib and I walked down the chute. I took a good look around. And I thought to myself, "Is that it? Is this all there is?"

Was I proud to have just laid down my first half? Hell, yes. But I failed to love, love, love the journey.

This time, I took a different approach. For the past 100+ days, I've been hugely present in all things marathon. The good, the bad, the ugly. Rip, sh*t or bust. Through every last blowout, breakdown, bad f*ing idea and breakthrough.

Today, I realized I'm already a winner. A winner for committing. A winner for putting in the miles. A winner for being way more present in my life.

And a winner for loving every last thing there is to love about this journey.

Today, I'm celebrating women, wisdom and the simple idea that we're all winners — just by showing up.

Last time I ran in Wyoming, I carried a bug on my front tooth for 8 freakin' miles. Unknowingly, of course. When I got back to the car, I flipped down the visor, smiled and thought, "For the love of all things holy, thank GOD there was no one else on the trail."

A Small Detour

I have never experienced the infamous runner's high.

This is the honest-to-God's truth. And I think I would know enough to know by now, right? Non-runners always ask, "Hey, do you get runner's high?" I'm like, "Hell no. But if that sh*t could kick in around mile 18 on race day, that would be cool."

I wondered this morning if runner's high was real. According to an article in the New York Times, it is.

The article stated researchers in Germany, using advances in neuroscience, reported in the journal Cerebral Cortex that the folk belief is true: Running does elicit a flood of endorphins in the brain. The endorphins are associated with mood changes, and the more endorphins a runner's body pumps out, the greater the effect.

My endorphin-o-meter must be broken. Or it's non-existent. Maybe altitude has killed it. It certainly hasn't yet registered anything positive or helpful when I'm laying the big boys down.

This morning, I took matters into my own hands: I created my own bad a** brand of runner's high.

Today was the first time in months I wasn't forced to rush. I slept until 6 a.m. (woo hoo!) and then drove over to the Platte River Parkway trail (an uber cool rails to trails conversion project) and put up a strong five miles.

You can tell I'm in Wyoming. As I'm sneaking out the front door of the hotel, the guy at the front counter says, "Hey, like your Cat Hat." I proudly replied, "Thank you, it's been with me for many-a-hard-earned miles."

At the trail head, I decide to run 2.5 miles out and back. Somewhere close to the half-way point, I look over and see an ancient, white, spiral slide.

In that moment, I had a decision to make. Either I could 1) Smile to myself and run right by, or 2) I could make a small detour and actually zip down that fantabulous piece of playground equipment.

I chose the detour.

As I climbed the 20-some-odd stairs to get to the top, I realize I haven't been on a slide in an equal number of years. Just before I push off, I offered up a quick prayer that the friction from the metal doesn't melt my freakin' pants to my legs. Or that it wouldn't tear a big a** hole in my backside.

I want to tell you that I flew Mach 12 all the way to the bottom. But I didn't. My legs are far too long. I was forced to tuck them around the center pole. It is probably the closest I will ever come to feeling like a stripper.

At the bottom, I took a peek around to make sure no one else was privy to my foolishness and I pressed on.

As I worked my way back to my car, I ran past the local roller-rink. I'm of the generation where it was cool as sh*t to tie two or three pairs of pom-poms to your skates and pretend you we're the queen of all things limbo.

Yeah, right. What once was hot definitely is no more. If I had to give the limbo a go today, either my a** or my 80s hair would hit that pesky bar for sure.

As my dawgs carried me back through the parking lot, I noticed someone waiting for me. (I'm not sure who was more scared, me or the deer.) Regardless, there was no Brook-meets-deer scrimmage. Thank you Jesus, because he'd have won.

Here are my lessons:

- Always carry a camera on the run. Take pictures of everything. It will help you remember where you've been.

- Get off the bloody path once in a while. I tend to land on the serious side of life, but sometimes feeling like a kid feels pretty freakin' awesome.

- Don't rely solely on endorphins. You can create your own bad-a** brand of runners high. You'll find what you're looking for in the least likely of places.

Today I'm celebrating super cool slides, old-fashioned skating rinks and the simple fact that we have the power to be as high as we choose.

So Damn Much Better

I'm nine days from burning down my first 26.2.

I'm kind of surprised I still have my wits about me. Of course, I'm still crying my head off every bloody day, but outside of that I'm of relatively sound mind.

Over the last few months, I've become keenly aware just how many people have hopped on my first marathon bus to give me high fives and shout a few hearty woot-woots.

A truckload.

My mom calls three times a week to ask about my miles. (Okay, she also wants to confirm I'm still a Christian after my recent metaphysical meanderings.) My sister-in-law has been cheering since the formation of the $1K Club. My BFF is heading down on race weekend to film a documentary of all things marathon. And Hubs has been picking up the slack every day while I run, blog and cry. (Not necessarily in that order.)

This just scratches the surface.

I have been blessed, (way more than I probably deserve), to have lots of people in my corner on this gig. Even if I came across a peep who didn't want to be in my corner, I freakin' stuffed them in there anyway.

Because I have my wits about me now, (and it's anybody's guess how long I'll be wrecked post-marathon), I'm starting to thank people.

First and foremost, I've been chewing on how to thank Midas. I think he deserves something awesome, and God knows the vet will hunt me down if I give him a freakin' cupcake. This is still TBD. Stand by.

Gifts and thank you notes went out this week to the peeps who went above and beyond with their support.

As for Hubs, that's still TBD, too. I'm thinking maybe a coupon book. He could redeem things like trip to liquor world, a home cooked meal, dinner with wife, dinner without bat sh*t wife, a full week without any crying. Hell, a full week without bat sh*t wife.

Hmmm.

All joking aside, today I'd like to thank YOU.

So many of you I haven't met (yet!). We've never shook hands, never snagged a cocktail or even a measly carb together. But you show up. You read the blog. You leave comments. You post notes and funny musings on Facebook. You e-mail me personal stories and race day photos.

You include me in YOUR journey.

I am humbled, honored and grateful.

More than 5,000 people cared enough to raise their hands and say, "Hell Yes! Brook, I'm all over supporting your crazy, soulful journey to 26.2." I've received hundreds of emails, Facebook messages and comments on the blog from sole sisters, (and a few bad-a** brothers), just to say, "You rock, you've got this, and I've got your back sister."

I've laughed my ever lovin' a** off with some of you. I've cried my eyes out with a few dozen more.

Thank you for coming along on this ride. Thank you not only for your encouragement, but for your unwavering, heart-felt support. Our friendship (whether virtual or eyeball-to-eyeball) made me so much stronger and this journey, so damn much better.

Today, I'm celebrating friendships, an off-the-charts fun factor and the faith that only good lies ahead for all of us.

I met a Caterpillar salesman in the lobby of my hotel this morning. By the time I'm done here, I may be driving home in a freakin' tractor.

FREE RESOURCE: I'd love to meet you and help you connect with other awesome sole sisters from all over the world. Stop by and say hey at www.Facebook.com/BrooksFirstMarathon.

Never A Lonely Mile

I have yet to run a lonely mile.

Many a runner smarter than me has said: "Sister, you'll run a truckload of lonely miles training for a marathon." This basically means an a** load of miles all by yourself.

When I first started this gig, I didn't know enough to get lonely on the trail. I was far too busy f*ing with my ear bud wires, water bottles and crappy Under Armour shirts.

Then came D.R., superstar support person of the planet. She's teammate No. 2 for Brook's First Marathon and inventor of the world's first pee machine. (Which we now lovingly refer to as the PrivaPee.) D.R. has been with me for the last fourteen weeks. Thank you Jesus.

Then Andi hopped on my marathon bus a few months back. She's probably been with me on seven or eight long runs. She cheers, supports and listens while I try to talk AND run at the same time, which I happen to be really f*ing bad at, btw. (It takes me 20 minutes to tell a 10 second story — thank God all you have is time when you're chasing the big numbers.)

And finally, a few other sole sisters have opted in along the way…to either 1) show their support or 2) lay down a new personal best. Today was no exception.

For months, my girlfriend Chris and I have been in-cahoots about running together. Today, it finally happened.

Here's how it all went down: Andi, D.R. and I hooked up early for one last round of hugs, hellos and a quick gift exchange. This was our last run together *before* the marathon.

I handed D.R. an orchid and a card. Andi handed her a Ziploc bag loaded to the gills with truffles. D.R. handed me a gift and asked me to not open it until *after* my race. I thought to myself, "Are you f*ing crazy? Do you know how hard it will be to leave a wrapped gift on my desk for eight freakin' days?"

We had a few minutes to kill before Chris arrived, so Andi and I decided to squeeze in a few extra miles.

Okay, let's be honest. Andi decided it's a brilliant idea to squeeze in a few pre-run miles. I, on the other hand, didn't want to be known as the girl who wouldn't. So I tagged along.

When we circle back to the starting line, Chris is ready to roll. She, too, came bearing gifts: hand-made snotty rags. Note: I am seriously considering another marathon just for the freakin' gifts. Things are getting borderline ridiculous 'round here. I love it.

Our intention was to put up eight miles this morning. But Chris pipes up and boldly says, "I think I'd like to go for 10."

So that's exactly what we did.

We ran, chatted, stretched, chatted, caught up with D.R., chatted. Before I knew it, we were back at the start line.

Chris put up a new personal best today. (10-miles. Yes!)

Here are my lessons:

- Again, I'm reminded there is magic in witnessing other people's PBs. Today, I was honored to watch Chris hit hers.

- Stay flexible with your training schedule. I set out to run eight miles today, but ended up doing more than 12. The girl I used to be would have gone bat sh*t. Hell, the girl I used to be wouldn't have been able to make that leap.

- I have run my a** off at work all week, and it showed today. Next week, I plan to eat well, hydrate up and sleep like I'm dying. I want to be the best version of myself on race day.

It hit me this morning that my time chasing 26.2 is almost up. A part of me is uber sad this item is almost off my bucket list. But the other part is crazy excited to finally run this marathon and see what's waiting for me on the other side.

Today I'm celebrating sisterhood, squeezing in extra miles and soon seeing the backside of all things marathon.

*My feet are so peeved today. The culprit? The sassy high-heeled shoes I just had to wear this week for work. Someone please remind me that sometimes, I do stupid sh*t.*

One Freakin' Day

Yesterday afternoon I was crabby.

Not just a little crabby, think full-on bat-sh*t mean a** crabby.

Most of it stems from feeling out of control. I'm sleep deprived. A ton of my to-do list items have been on the back burner for far too long. And I had to make a trip to the dreaded grocery store. I hate that sh*t.

While I was out mowing down endless errands, I whispered to Hubs, "I'm tired of running." He looks at me with a raised brow as if to say, "Go on."

Okay, maybe he didn't exactly mean, "Go on." Maybe it was the, "Is this where you get all weird and weepy?" look. Either way, I took it as an invitation to continue.

I confessed, "It feels like all I've done for the last 18 weeks is run and run and run. I'd love one freakin' day where I can putz around my kitchen in my PJs and get my life somewhat back in order."

I'm sharing this in case you, too, have times during training where you're like, "F it. I'm over all of this. I'm going to lay in bed for a week. Or take a month off and sit my a** beach side in a foreign country. Or I'm going to get in my car and drive to a faraway land to escape this nonsense." It's normal. I think. Even if it's not, consider this permission to do it anyway.*

Hub's reply was simple: "Then take your one freakin' day." I promised to chew on it. After all, I doubted the answer could be that easy.

After surviving the mass of those who insist on running errands at the same place and time as I do, I returned home, snagged half a cocktail and laid down for a 33-minute nap. I was by no stretch a new woman. But there was a *noticeable* improvement.

We had friends over for dinner last night. It was a red meat and cosmo throw down of epic proportions. We used the only cloth napkins I own. We ate in the formal dining room. We gorged on rib eyes, baked potatoes, oodles of tapas and homemade apple crisp.

My sour mood didn't stand a chance.

This morning I slept until 6:30 a.m. I took Midas on a short walk. I came home, stripped the bed, started laundry and unloaded the dishwasher. (You know, all the sexy sh*t you have to do just to survive.)

The plan was a run and a hike, but instead, I opted to putz around my kitchen. After mindlessly moving around for some unknown amount of time, I threw on my grubby clothes and went to war with my yard. I pulled and sprayed weeds for hours. Before calling it a day, Hubs and I pulled out the patio furniture. Nothing signals summer like an outdoor dining room.

Here is my lesson: Ever since I started training, I've been in a perpetual state of recommitting. I've had to recommit (daily!) to nutrition. Recommit to running. Recommit to the journey. The process. The very reason I'm doing this in the first place. There's no shame in re-committing. The shame would be if I didn't.

So, the rest of the day I stayed on easy street. I called my Mom to wish her Happy Mother's Day. Hubs grilled up burgers and we toasted with frozen margaritas. I sat my a** in my favorite patio chair and soaked up some much-needed sun.

Today, I'm celebrating foreign countries, faraway lands and the simple fact I finally stole my one freakin' day.

Here's my secret-secret, easy-peasy margarita recipe: 1 can of beer, 1 can of 7 Up, 1 can of frozen limeade and 1 can of tequila (use the empty limeade can). Stir. Place in freezer overnight. Pull out of freezer. Put in glass. Start sipping. Love your life.

I've learned some pretty awesome lessons on this journey.

This weekend, I wrote out almost 200 things I've learned so far on this wild a** ride. Some were outrageous. Others were minuscule. A few brought tears to my eyes. Others had me clutching my side and rolling around on the floor with laughter. There's simply no denying it: I've done some crazy, stupid sh*t over the course of the last few months.

I thought I'd share my "best of" list, so you can 1) laugh your ever lovin' head off; 2) avoid a few ridiculous, costly mistakes; and/or 3) use these as a guide when mapping out your training plan.

Let's roll ...

BK's Top 50 Marathon + Life Lessons

1. Never head out for a long run within an hour after you eat. EVER.

2. If you're not having fun, don't do it.

3. Not every piece of gear you buy will be a brilliant purchase.

4. Every day, at least one body part will scream, "I don't want to get on the f*ing marathon bus today." Shove 'em on there anyway.

5. You cannot train for a marathon on Cheetos, cinnamon rolls and margaritas alone.

6. Get quiet. You'll find what you're looking for in the silence.

7. You will experience chafing. Only God knows where.

8. Not all sports bras play fair.

9. Sh*t happens. Be smart (and strategic!) about safety.

10. Buy an armband. A Ziploc bag between your girls is a damn bad plan.

11. Start a book of awesome. Write down five reasons a day it's awesome to be YOU.

12. Sometimes, the most productive thing you can do is relax.

13. Marathon training is tough at the beginning, f*ing messy in the middle and awesome at the end.

14. You won't lose use of your faculties if your ear buds shock the *inside* of your ears.

15. Set up a magic P.O. Box. Only share the address with super cool peeps.

16. Sometimes your body isn't kidding. It simply must stop to pee.

17. Don't layer Under Armour shirts.

18. Compression socks aren't just for peeps with diabetes.

19. Trust you will have exactly what you need when you need it.

20. When in doubt, go back to your tried and true gear. No one gives a sh*t if it's ancient or ugly.

21. Should your brain lose contact with your legs, your legs will know what to do.

22. Expensive doesn't equal best.

23. The magic happens during new miles. (Distances you've never run before.)

24. Some days, your "Be a Marathoner" mood will be MIA.

25. If it's not an absolute yes, it's a hell no.

26. Know when to fold 'em. Some long runs are sh*t storms. If you have to call a run, call it.

27. The difference between a runner and a mature runner is the willingness to take rest days.

28. Finishing = Winning.

29. Apple can take you around the world and down memory lane in 43 minutes.

30. Pride is ENOUGH.

31. Don't run your first marathon for time. Run it for you.

32. Hands down, one Clif Bar in your purse is not enough.

33. Be nice to the airline peeps. They just might save your a**.

34. Chocolate, vodka and red meat can cure anything.

35. Your itty bitty sh*tty committee is made up of world-class a** holes. You don't have to listen.

36. When you say "YES!" to life, life will say "YES!" to you.

37. Your doctor's office will not tell you you're *dying* in an email.

38. There are peeps in the world who will hold your hand, kick your a** or simply offer their cheering services because they can.

39. When you have less-than-solid long runs week after week, you will question if you should be doing this. Press on.

40. Be flexible with your training schedule. Get while the gettin' is good.

41. Cheer up. It took someone in Honolulu over 14 freakin' hours to run a marathon.

42. Acupuncture does not hurt. But it can totally p*ss off your Chi.

43. No one said training for a marathon is a modest or dainty endeavor.

44. When your body checks out, your mind and your heart will carry you home.

45. Pay it forward. Witnessing someone else's journey to the finish line is magic.

46. The kindest thing you can do for yourself is acknowledge how far you've come.

47. Cute as sh*t matters. Just make sure you test that cute as sh*t gear before race day.

48. Hold on to your love of running for dear life. It will bring you back if you happen to lose your way.

49. Endorphins haven't cornered the market on runner's high. Create your own bad a** version.

50. There is no shame in having to recommit daily. The shame would be if we didn't.

Today I'm celebrating lessons learned, leaning in and laughing out freakin' loud.

Midas and I put up four miles today. We didn't break any world records but the weather was fantabulous.

Race Day Rules

I have never, ever read through race day rules.

You know, that crazy, 800-page packet of information they include with your race registration. The cans and can'ts, dos and don'ts. How to ramp up your runner's etiquette so you don't get spit on, cussed at or mowed down by the *real* runners hoping to take home prize money.

I can't say I'm overly-mindful about etiquette. It's not that I run all over the place with my rude pants-a-flashing, but I tend to think that because I'm a nice, conscientious, friendly sort of gal, I can generally navigate any situation life throws my way.

But listen. Running a marathon is the big leagues. So in addition to actually running 26.2 miles on race day, I thought I'd better research what's expected of my behavior, too.

I spent an hour last night investigating race-day rules. Some of what I read freakin' shocked me.

I was thinking, "Seriously? You have to tell people that? They don't already know not to smoke cigarettes or talk on their cell phone while running?" Yeah. Um, I definitely plan to pull over around mile 15, give my dawgs a much-needed break, light a ciggie, guzzle a cocktail and call my Mother.

But that was only the beginning. Apparently, there is an entire set of rules I was meant to uncover.

Rule #1 -- SPITTING and POWER SNOTTING.

Experts say if you must spit, aim it downward in a slight diagonal direction to avoid splashing or hitting other runners. Same goes for power snotting. Take a quick peek around to make sure no one is within target range. (You can Google power snotting videos to perfect your technique.)

Listen. For one, if I am spit or snotted upon on race day, what I'll do depends on where I am on the course. If it's mile four, you're in for the fight of your life. If it's mile 25, f* it. Spit and/or snot on with your bad self.

Rule #2 -- SURGING.

The info I found warned, "Don't cut another runner off and then slow down once you're in front of them."

For a second I got confused. Am I reading the Colorado Department of Transportation Handbook for How to Be a Damn Bad Driver or am I reading the rules for running a marathon? Either way, it's not likely I'll pass too many peeps on race day, so duly noted.

Rule #3 -- WATER STATIONS.

Note: This is where I started to flip out. Every article I read on how to snag a freakin' Dixie Cup off of a plastic table made collecting water sound more difficult than giving birth.

Here are the CLIFFS NOTES for the highly technical process of snatching a drink on race day:

Figure out you're thirsty. (Brilliant.) Look ahead and find the nearest water station. Without cutting anyone off, tell your brain to tell your dawgs it's time to move curbside. While making your way over, tell your brain to tell your arm to jut straight out to signal your innards need a freakin' drink. Listen closely for the peeps who shout "water!" or "Gatorade!" In your best outside voice, holler back what you want. Grab your drink and move immediately back to the middle of the road. For the love of all things holy...do not cut anyone off. Take a drink. Offer up thanks someone was crazy enough to volunteer for that freakin' gig. Toss your cup to the side. Press onward.

Rule #4 -- THE CORRALS.

Do not, under any circumstance, sneak into a corral where you do not belong. Corrals are there to keep the fast runners separate from those of us who are slow as sh*t. You'd hate to get trampled crossing the start line for hell's sake.

Rule #5 -- THE BIB.

For one, don't wear someone else's bib. (If I steal a bib, I will make sure I steal one from a Kenyan. And that he or she steals mine.) Second, pin your bib, using all four safety pins, to the front of your shirt. Not your back, not your a**, not your shorts. And finally, don't run a race without a bib. (They call this to Bandit a Race -- when you run without paying.)

Who knew there were so many stinkin' rules around the damn bib?

Rule # 6 -- THANK THE VOLUNTEERS.

This is as easy as a high five, a woot woot, or a simple thank you. There are hundreds of peeps giving up their entire day to make sure you have what you need to finish the race.

Note: I personally seek out every police officer on the course and give 'em a high-five. It's the only time in your freakin' life where you know for sure they aren't looking for you. It's also one of the only times when an officer of the law will crack a smile.

Are there at least 100 more rules to read through? Sure. Do I feel like I've got my sh*t together for race day? Absofreakinlutely.

Because now I know how to spit and power snot. (I watched the videos.) I know what I'll do if I'm spit or snotted upon. If I have the opportunity to surge, (which isn't likely), I'll know to keep truckin'. I will tell my brain to tell my dawgs that we're to creep up on the water station with ease and grace. I'll also try not to cut anyone off. Ever. I'll keep to myself in the, "We're slow as sh*t" corral pre-race. I'll lovingly pin my bib, (or the one I stole from a Kenyan), on the front of my shirt. And finally, I'll high-five every single police officer I see for 26.2 long, treacherous miles in hopes of seeing a few of them smile.

We hiked last night. Midas totally scored. Think all things ponds, dirt and outdoors.

I love, love, love having girlfriends.

For a long time, I didn't bother hanging out with women. I thought they, (we, whatever), were catty and bitchy. But the older I get, the smarter I've become. I've come to rely on other women's wisdom, insights and war stories to help navigate my life.

Most of my girlfriends are older than I am, which means nearly all of them are 1) rounding the corner on menopause; or 2) they're smack dab in the middle of that ugly, sh*tty mess.

Last week, I was chatting up a good friend from L.A. She was bellyaching about how bitchy she's been and how these days, she's full-on bat sh*t three weeks out of every four.

A few days later another girlfriend shared in grave detail everything there is to know about hot flashes. She can't sleep. She sweats her a** off several times a day. She's battling the bulge (i.e. weight gain) and failing miserably. She's holding on to her sanity for dear freakin' life.

And I'm thinking, "Holy f. So let me get this straight. You spend your entire life striving for wisdom, beauty and brilliance. When you finally start to get a clue about how all this sh*t works, your body blows out and betrays you. I can't wait.*

I love that women share their genius.

While you can't possibly know how things will affect you until you experience them for yourself, it is helpful to know what may be lurking around the next curve. This goes for anything: hot flashes, divorce, childbirth, the death of your dog, whatever. (Yes, I recently had a lengthy conversation about what it's like to put your dog down. F*ing terrible.)

The same goes for running a marathon.

Hundreds of women have shared (with me!) their wisdom about what to expect while training for my first marathon. They've also warned me of pitfalls and how it will feel to cross the finish line. I have sat at my desk and cried my ever lovin' eyes out at least a dozen times reading their stories.

Don't get me wrong, I've laughed too. Seems I'm not the only girl on the planet who does some crazy, ridiculous sh*t. Thank you, Jesus.

Here's just a small bit of what other marathoners have shared:

"The race was so much harder than I ever imagined. By the last seven miles, I'm doing math in my head, trying to figure out if we can still meet our goal. It's hard to do math at that point. I had a little emotional breakdown at mile 25 marker, but when I saw my husband at the finish line taking pictures, I lost it. I ran with a friend (was also her first) and I think we've bonded for life."

#####

"When I hit the wall at mile 20 it became mind over matter. At that point, I realized you can do a lot more than you think. It's not our bodies that stop us; it's our minds. And after I got my mind on track, the last 6.2 were amazing."

#####

"I ran my first marathon last year and hit my wall at mile 18. Everything hurt. My legs, my feet, my arms, I wanted to cry I was so frustrated! But I thought to myself, "I'm tougher than this," and kept going. As soon as I saw the finish line and my family and friends cheering me on, I knew in my heart it was all worth it."

#####

"I cried as I got through the finish line. Like *ugly* cried. I was one of the last few who finished. But I DNC; I finished!"

#####

"I have to say, it's great being an all the way girl! I enjoyed it fully and learned a lot. Don't over think it. Just show up, lay it all down on the road and enjoy it."

#####

After reading these notes, who doesn't' want to burn down their first 26.2?

With a few short days to go, the only thing left to wonder is, "Will I finish?"

Hey, until you actually run your first marathon, you don't KNOW. And how could you, you've never done it before, right?

But thanks to a few wise women, I now know what may be waiting for me on Sunday. An emotional breakdown. (Or five!) Hitting the wall. Tons of pictures. Mind over matter. Feet, legs and arms that ache, ache, ache. A good, UGLY cry.

And the idea that even if sh*t isn't pretty on race day; it just might be pretty awesome.

*I just got off the phone with my BFF. She said, "Brook, this is a BFD." I'm like, "What? Another word runner's use that I don't know?" She comes back with, "Big F*ing Deal." She's right.*

Love/Hate Relationship

I have a love/hate relationship with running.

Most people think I love, love, love to run. When you mention to anyone you're training for a marathon, they automatically go to a place of, "Oh! Sh*t! No kidding! You're one of those crazy a** blonde chicks rockin' the ponytail and the cute skirt. You were probably born wearing ASICS. I bet this sh*t comes easy for you because you're all sorts of twiggy."

Then they whisper behind my back, "What a freakin' dumb a**."

(Sometimes I tell myself the same thing so no worries.)

This morning, I woke up and every last cell in my body begged, "For the love of all things holy sister. Do we have to do this? Again? Love! Rest! How about a cocktail and a cinnamon roll for breakfast. Why don't we lounge around in our robe for an hour or two and watch re-runs of The Voice ..." Not today. I threw on my gear and out the door I went. (4 miles.)

There's a lot about running I love. There are likely an equal number of things I don't. Here's what puts me sideways when it comes to rockin' the road:

- When my ear bud wires try to strangle me first thing every stinkin' morning.

- When my favorite sports bra is dirty.

- How many loads of laundry I do each week so my favorite running clothes are clean.

- Calling a long run because some part of my body refuses to get in the game.

- Waking up wondering how in the hell I managed to get run over by a Mack Truck in the night.

- Buying cute as sh*t gear, only to suffer a terrible case of buyer's remorse.

- The two-week recovery period after a 22 mile throw down.

- Worrying about safety because some people are f*ing crazy.

- That the human body simply cannot go and go and go without rest.

- Chaffing.

- That pedicures only last one week before the polish starts to chip.

- When every freakin' bathroom along the route is closed.

- When your itty bitty sh*tty committee screams, "You haven't done enough!" when you know damn good and well you have.

All these things aside, I keep coming back for more. Because truth be told, no matter how many things put me sideways, what I love about running far outweighs what I don't.

Here's what I totally dig about rockin' the road:

- Eating a house with zero consequence.

- The sisterhood and camaraderie.

- Feeling like a freakin' warrior.

- New personal bests.

- Laying down a long run and living to tell about it.

- Cute as sh*t gear. (Before you learn it was a damn bad idea.)

- Skinny jeans.

- Doing what you said you'd do, even when it 1000% sucks.

- Running gives you a hall pass to wear anything you choose.

- The simple fact that when you find your way through your baggage and bull sh*t, there is always a breakthrough.

- How it changes you as a person and who you become in the process.

Many-a-time running has kicked my a**, broken my heart and snatched my pride. But it always gives far more than it takes.

I was relatively unemotional this week.

This kind of surprised me. For months, I've laughed my head off, cried my eyes out and turned myself inside out about every last thing there was to be inside out about. But this week? Not so much. I've had no major breakdowns. No ugly "burst into bat sh*t" episodes. No mean a**, crabby full-blown catastrophes.

Until yesterday.

All week, behind the scenes, I've been strategizing race day. Here's what that looks like: Running without my Cat Hat to see if I can run hat-less on Sunday. It's a go.

Final testing race day attire. The dress? Yeah. Um, it's out. It's perfect for a 10k, or maybe even a half. But I know I'd chafe from here to Shinola over 26.2 miles. No freakin' way. But make no mistake; I will wear a skirt on race day.

Organizing logistics. This included setting up text message alerts so peeps know where I am on the course and when to expect me. Everyone who is planning to hold their breath at the finish line has been emailed my ETA and post-race party plans.

Fielding phone calls, emails and text messages. Every communication tool I own is currently on overdrive. Peeps want to know, "How are you? What's up? How do you feel? Are you ready?"

Late yesterday afternoon, I scooted across town for one last massage. It was my final attempt at coercing/begging my muscles to do what I'm *asking* them to do on Sunday.

On the way over, I popped into Sports Authority to snag new sun sleeves. A few weeks back, I ordered a black pair online. Yeah. Right. They won't stay up on my bulging pipes. (I think my biceps have shrunk. Seriously.)

On my drive home from a masterful kneading of all things muscle, I had a full-blown anxiety attack.

What the f* am I doing? Why am I doing this? What if I can't? What if I don't finish? I must be a total dumb a**. Who freakin' does this? Better yet, who f*ing shares this experience with thousands of people? For the love of all things holy sister, you're now the star of an epic, full-blown, one-woman sh*t show.

I'd like to tell you the attack was fleeting, but it hung around all night. I knew I needed to check the f* out for a few hours. So I grabbed the latest copy of O Magazine and went on the hunt for a little inspiration.

I found it. (Thank you Oprah, for puttin' up time and time again.)

In the June 2013 issue, Oprah interviews Brene Brown, Ph.D., author of the best-seller *Daring Greatly*. In the interview, Brown shares that she found the title of her book in a quote from Theodore Roosevelt:

"It is not the critic who counts; not the man who points out how the strong man stumbles, or where the doer of deeds could have done them better. The credit belongs to the man who is actually in the arena, whose face is marred by dust and sweat and blood; who strives valiantly; who errs...[and] if he fails, at least fails while daring greatly."

That's who I want to be. The (wo)man in the arena.

This adventure isn't about winning. It isn't about what other people think. It's about showing up, being seen and sharing the truth of the experience -- good, bad or indifferent. My face has definitely been marred by proverbial dust, sweat and blood. But I'm in the arena, baby. And that alone is the freakin' big leagues.

Today, I'm celebrating credit, courage and the final, final countdown.

I'm off to pick up my bib today! I got tears in my eyes when they sent the email that said: BIB number # 759, BROOK KREDER, for the MARATHON race. Here we go...

Rip, Sh*t or Bust

I bet I've developed quite a reputation around my town.

Thank God I don't live in a community of 1,500, or I'd have been shackled in the bat sh*t house long ago. With a daily commitment to all things blogging, I've become a photo journalist of epic proportions, which is another way of saying I'm constantly begging people to hop on my bus, scoot in a little closer and have their picture taken with this wanna-be-marathoner.

Yesterday's bib pick up was no exception.

*I think packet pick up sucks. Race organizers often make you trek all the way downtown (or somewhere at least 45 minutes from your house), find parking and fight your way through a mass of other people crazy enough to chase the same finish line. Someone should tell them we'd be happy to pay $10 extra dollars to have that sh*t shipped to our house.*

During pick up, they also force you through a health and wellness expo.

So yesterday, I sampled organic orange juice. I listened to a 10-minute pitch about why I should switch socks. (Talk about being late to the party.) I snagged two packets of chocolate protein powder. And I was lucky enough to meet the head medic at the beer wristband station. Thank you, Jesus.

His name is Stewart.

When he told me he was the head medic, I snatched his hand. I looked him dead in the eye and recited my name, my address and my social security number. I told him I'm allergic to codeine, and I encouraged him to remember my face in the off chance we meet in his tent tomorrow. He promised he would.

Then I moved over to pick up my official marathon t-shirt. That's where I met Sue Ellen.

She volunteers to work dozens of races each year. She was super friendly and more than willing to throw down about all things t-shirt. (She's one I had to coerce to get on the picture bus, but after telling her this is my first marathon, she couldn't help but oblige.) Before we left her table, Andi and I high-fived and thanked her.

One of my last stops was the Skirt Sport booth. That's where I met Susannah. She gave me a crack at spinning their "wheel of good fortune" for up to $10 off my new skirt.

I walked away with a Twix Bar. Sh*t. But, I made a new friend. And she's just starting to train for her first marathon - woot!

Note: The only group I did not snap a picture of were the fire fighters lubed up and lounging in their booth. I was so distracted I simply forgot. (I know!) But all 12 of them were young and strong, and their charm-o-meters were off the freakin' charts. I have to be honest; I'm a little peeved their half-neked bodies will be nowhere near the marathon course. They've reserved their bewitchery for the half marathon peeps.

Here's how the rest of my day went:

- A trip to the grocery store. (You know I hate that sh*t.)

- A quick spot clean of my house. (I don't think I'll be able to walk for a week, better do it today.)

- Washed my race day outfit. (I tested it one last time on my run this morning.)

- Race day signs. My BFF and I busted out the markers to show our support for other sole sisters at the finish line.

The day ushered in a few tears and a truckload of laughs.

But here's what I know for sure: The next time I sit down to write, I will be a marathoner.

Too Tough To Kill

Now I know. I'm too tough to kill.

This, of course, is another way of saying yes baby, I burned down 26.2 miles this morning. But make no mistake. I beat the hell out of myself chasing those miles.

Running a marathon is so damn much harder than people tell you. Even if someone did tell you, there is no way you could fathom what's in store until you experience it yourself.

I ran my FIRST marathon in 4 hours, 42 minutes and 20 seconds.

Am I happy with that number? Absofreakinlutely. Do I have any desire (today) to recommit to another marathon? F* no.

Listen. I flipped Hubs off at mile 20. My dawgs divorced me at mile 22. My heart hopped out of my ever lovin' chest at the finish line. And my mouth would not stop spewing cuss words. It was freakin' awesome.

I promise you'll get the unedited, blow-by-blow of all things marathon ASAP. (Not to complain, but I'm exhausted, uber sunburned and I need a vodka tonic and a good night sleep before sharing.)

Thank you for the love, encouragement, texts, emails and phone calls today. Words cannot express how honored and grateful I am for YOU, your support and our friendship.

A few months ago, I found this quote online about what it feels like to run a marathon. Today, it sums things up perfectly:

"At mile 20, I thought I was dead. At mile 22, I wished I were dead. At mile 24, I knew I was dead. At mile 26.2, I realized I had become too tough to kill." -- Anonymous

Today, I'm celebrating the backside of all things marathon. (And you should see the view! It's so damn much better than I ever thought it would be!)

229

Blow By Blow

Let's take it from the top.

I woke up in the middle of the night last night parched and starving. Around 4 a.m., I knew there was no way on God's green earth I was going back to sleep, so I threw on my Cat Hat, hooked Midas to his leash and we headed out for a two mile schlep around the neighborhood. (John Wayne ain't got nothing on my swagger today.)

While limping along, I offered up a ton of thanks for finishing my first marathon in what I consider a respectable amount of time. Not only that, but I celebrated the fact that I simply survived the freakin' ordeal. (I swear, it blows my mind this sh*t doesn't kill me.)

Yesterday's throw down will be blistered in my mind until I go to the grave. Not only did I burn more calories in five hours than I probably do in a freakin' week, but I pushed myself farther (and harder!) than I ever thought possible.

*Grab a snack and get comfortable...what I'm sharing today is the blow-by-blow, (from my perspective of course), of what it's really like to chase 26.2 long, treacherous, mean-spirited, take no prisoner, bad a** miles.*

No one tells you, in the fine print or otherwise, that when your race starts at 6 a.m. you have no choice but to get up in the middle of the freakin' night to eat, pull your sh*t together, get dressed and drive 35 miles to make the start line on time.

I made it to my corral with several minutes to spare, which is another way of saying there was plenty of time for high-fives, ugly pictures and busting out my best singing voice for the National Anthem.

We also had a few moments of silence for Boston, which was inspiring and saddening all in the same breath.

At 6:06 a.m. I rolled over the starting line of my first marathon.

Let me tell you, peeps were zipping by me right out of the gate and I was thinking, "WTF? Am I in the right corral? Did I misjudge my time? Should I pick up the pace? Try to trip a few of them? Throw in the towel altogether and go snag a mean a** breakfast?"

I let them zoom by, hoping I'd catch them later when their legs blew out.

The first five miles were easy peasy. (Thank you, Jesus.) At mile five, the course veered into a fire station. Unfortunately, all of the men were fully clothed, but there is something very motivating about blowing by 50 men in uniform whose sole purpose is to cheer for you.

I tore out the other side of that firehouse and hastily ripped off my t-shirt. I had officially entered "warrior zone."

At mile nine, out of the corner of my eye, I see D.R. and her husband. She is holding a bright a** fluorescent yellow sign with my name plastered on the front in big, black, bold letters.

I hopped off the trail, snagged a hug and a high five, and pressed on.

At mile 14, I veered curbside and broke out a Clif Bar. That's also when Self and I had a one-person pep talk. "Self," I said, "You got this. You feel good. You're hydrated. You look cute as sh*t. We're on the downhill slide of all things marathon, sister. Keep those legs a movin'."

At mile 18, the sun reared its ugly head.

And that is when the going got tough. I see two peeps standing on a median in the middle of the street and I roll their way. I rip out an ear bud and holler, "What time is it?" They shout back, "8:52 a.m." Two things go through my mind. The first is, "Sh*t! Check me out! I'm running sub 10-minute miles! Freakin' awesome!" That's also when my brain told my dawgs we'd been pounding pavement for almost 3 hours with at least another 90 minutes to go.

Double sh*ts.

I run the next two miles with the sun blasting its wicked rays directly on my forehead. Just before mile 20, I look over and see Collette, from Boulder Running Company, standing on the sidelines.

"Collette!" I cry (like she can save me). She cheers, "Brook! OMG! How is your first marathon treating you?" "Holy Christ," I say. "This sh*t is so much worse than I ever imagined." She comes back with, "You got this sister, I'm rooting for you. Swing by the store this week and tell me all about it." I promised I would, and again, I pressed on.

At mile 20, I see a hydration station. I selfishly grab a Gatorade and a water.

That was when sh*t started to get freakin' brutal. Not just, "Oh, this kind-of sucks." Think, "Oh f*! What am I doing and why did I ever think chasing 26.2 miles was a good idea? Who talked me in to this? Where are they now? I'm so out of here. To hell with 26; 20 is plenty."

As I walk up the hill suckling a water cup, I see Hubs. He has the camera pointed directly at me. That's when I stick my middle finger straight in the air. There was no mistaking what I meant.

*Listen. At this point, I was tired and hungry. The sun was doing its best to fry me. My feet were deeply p*ssed. My armband was trying valiantly to chew a hole the size of a silver dollar in my bicep. And I was just a little f*ing grouchy.*

He said, "You're doing great. What do you need? You good?"

In a voice that was nothing short of snarky I replied, "I'm fine. But a new pair of legs and a cocktail would be cool." We chatted for around 60 seconds and I'm ready to roll again.

One thing I've not yet mentioned: Hubs rode his bicycle to catch me at different locations on the course. I probably saw him four or five times yesterday while I was pounding pavement. It was a damn nice thing for him to do.

As I'm chasing mile marker 21, he rolled up next to me on his bike and asked (again!) if I needed anything.

I whispered, "Water."

At this point, to say I felt a little deflated is the understatement of the century. So he stopped and let me pull his bottle out of the backpack. I guzzled at least half. (I would have drunk more, but I was afraid I'd puke.)

He rode next to me for a few hundred yards and gave my confidence a much-needed boost.

"I'll see you at the finish," he smiled. And I'm back in the game.

I blew through mile 21.

I looked around and told myself, "Only 5.2 miles to go girl. You can run five miles in your f*ing sleep. Hunker down, bust out your A-game, and put this b*tch to bed."

At mile 22, I got all kinds of p*ssed off.

I suppose I came to a fork in the road. Either I could cry and flail around on the ground, or I could get p*ssed and let anger carry me home. I can't say I consciously chose anger; it was just what showed up. It worked.

I missed mile marker 23 altogether. (I.e., I didn't see the sign.)

So I ran and ran and ran and it felt like the damn longest mile I'd ever run in my life. (Turns out it was.)

I finally saw mile marker 24. Thank you, Jesus.

Again, I stopped for a drink. I stretched out my legs. And I told myself, "Only 2.2 miles to go. You can freakin' *crawl* that far if you have to. Let's get this done."

I took off in a slow jog. By now, every stinkin' part of my body has 1000 percent checked the f* out. I kept asking myself, (over and over), "Why do you want to walk? What hurts? Your legs? Your lungs? Your heart? Your feet? Tell me what hurts and we'll work something out."

Nothing hurt. It was just a fatigue that is totally indescribable.

I made it to mile 25 and honest to God, I started to walk. I swear on my mother's life I walked at least a half a mile between miles 25 and 26. I didn't care. My feet were so freakin' heavy, I was afraid I'd trip myself and take a digger. But don't let me fool you; my eyes were on full alert for a mere glimpse of that finish line. (I didn't want anyone to "see" me walking; my ego was obviously still intact.)

At mile 25.5, I pulled up my big girl britches and we carried that b*tch the rest of the way home.

I threw my arms in the air and took my final steps over the finish line. I was in shock. A few feet into the chute, a fire fighter placed the medal around my neck.

Listen. The last thing on earth I needed in that moment was a hot stranger leaning in to catch a whiff. Can't a girl keep her pride?

Ten steps later, I tore the medal clean off because it felt far too heavy for my weary bones.

One of the volunteers handed me a bottle of water. I selfishly asked for a second. She told me no. Seriously?!

I then snagged some trail mix, a bagel and half of a banana. I could not get that sh*t down my throat fast enough.

I exited the chute and didn't see my peeps. So I wandered around like a lost child until I found a tree that could hold me. I then propped my a** against the trunk, closed my eyes and rested.

It took me 10 minutes to connect with my finish-line party. But it was like Christmas morning when I did. There were plenty of high fives, hugs, tears, signs, flowers and a-freakin'-mens to go round.

And that's when it finally hit me.

Holy Cripes. I just ran a f*ing MARATHON.

Today I'm celebrating friends, the finish line and the fantastic feeling of finally being able to say, "I am a marathoner."

We had a rockin' after party yesterday, and I caught up with a few sole sisters who ran the half. They showered before heading out in public...I should take lessons.

FREE RESOURCE: Go to www.MarathonTrainingTools.com to get instant, VIP access to the raw, unedited footage of my finish line video!

I haven't run since the marathon.

Well, that's not exactly true. I ran 25 steps this morning up a hill just to test sh*t out. My body was like, "Yeah. Um, right. Not today bad-a**." So Midas and I strolled around the neighborhood. (Perhaps stroll is still too strong a word.)

All things considered, I feel surprisingly good. Actually, I feel a hell of a lot better than I did after my 22-miler a few weeks ago. Thank you, Jesus.

For the last few days, I've been blissing on all things post-marathon. I finally washed my car. It was so freakin' filthy the peeps at the car wash threatened to charge me double. (No joke.)

I also shared the raw, unedited footage of my finish line video. While I didn't burst into tears crossing the finish line, the feedback I received was enough to make me cry.

Yesterday afternoon, I ate my way through half a jar of salsa and an entire bag of tortilla chips. It got all kinds of ugly up in here: Think salt and chip explosion. Before I knew it, I looked down and noticed I'd reached the bottom of the chip bag. Oh f*. (It was *not* my proudest moment.)

That's when it h it me. "My Gawd. If I keep this up, I'll have no choice but to run marathons for the rest of my ever lovin' life. It may be the only way to keep up with my freakin' mouth."

So, in addition to washing my car, hitting the grocery store and writing checks to all the peeps I owe money to, I also popped into my local running store to pick up my next race day packet.

Yep. You heard right. I'm running a 10k in four days.

I seriously haven't thought about this race since I registered a few months back. And I certainly didn't realize it was only eight days after my first marathon. When an email reminder arrived yesterday I thought, OMG. What the f* have I done?

In a panic, I immediately called Andi -- my gal Friday for all things running.

I inquired, "Is this a bad idea? What should I expect? Will it kill me? Will it wind up being a one-woman sh*t show? Should I forfeit my registration fee and lay around on my a** eating ice cream instead?"

She said she thinks I'll be fine. But she also said it probably won't be a PR. (At this stage, who cares?! That's seriously the last thing on my mind.) What's cool about a 10k is it's short enough to take my new cute as sh*t dress for a test drive.

So have I been busy since burning down 26.2 miles? Yep.

But not *so* stinkin' busy that I haven't spent time reflecting on my big day.

The No. 1 thing I've chewed on is what I could have done differently, during training, to make the last five miles of the marathon easier. (Let's be honest, that's where sh*t got messy.) I've identified what I believe to be my two major f* ups. When I can put these mistakes into words, I'll share.

So, I'm officially living in the gap. I have one foot in the past, (i.e. living the bliss of simply surviving a marathon), and one foot in the future, (i.e. what's next, what's next, what's next?).

For now, I'll continue to search for the balance between celebrating my accomplishment and not resting on my laurels.

And I'll do my best to like it.

######

Epilogue

So there it is: The no b.s., absolute truth about training for your first marathon.

Now you know, it's not easy. The truth is, it's f*ing hard. And kind of ugly. And really freakin' messy.

But, so totally doable.

If you're wondering if you can run a marathon, I'm here to tell you – Yes, you can. But first, you have to *decide*. Because at the end of the day, the only person responsible for running the miles and reaching the finish line is YOU.

Chasing 26.2 miles is no joke. It's not a half-a** endeavor. It will break your heart, snatch your pride, chew you up, break you down and leave you beggin' for your ever-lovin' life.

But it will heal whatever it is in your life that you're ready to heal.

So if you crave something bigger, and you know more awaits you, then dig in. Because the backside of all things marathon is f*ing magic.

ONWARD!

Brook Kreder
Marathoner!
www.BrookKreder.com

P.S. Hey – one last thing. It's true, only you can run your miles. But you don't have to do it alone. Join the conversation at www.Facebook.com/BrooksFirstMarathon.com. I promise there are thousands of other sole sisters who will have your back. XOXO.

*P.P.S. The journey continues! (Either I'm a total dumb a** or wickedly brilliant.) To snag a front row seat on my next adventure, move your mouse over to www.BrookKreder.com. See you there!*

28915535R00129